Interior Architecture and Decoration

Alain Demachy

Interior Architecture and Decoration

William Morrow & Company, Inc.   New York

Translated from the French:
Architecture d'Intérieur et Décoration

Layout: Studio S + T, Lausanne
French text: Laurence Buffet-Challié
English translation: J. A. Underwood

Library of Congress Catalog Card
Number 74-11646
ISBN 0–688–00281–1

Printed in Switzerland

Contents

Part One

To create a framework to accommodate the occupants' life-style, you must have a rational basis, i.e., certain architectural data.

I

Drawing up a plan

Whether the dwelling to be designed is a house or an apartment, one component of success is to start out with an objective approach.

First take account of the number of inhabitants, together with their ages and activities. Then analyse their life-style—whether it is centred on the family or whether it is primarily social. To create a framework to accommodate that life-style, you must have a rational basis, i.e., certain architectural data. A disjointed piece of architecture, whether ancient or modern, can never, however attractive in principle, be made pleasant and harmonious to live in. It may be quaint, amusing, unusual, and all the rest of it. It makes no difference... One cannot spend one's life in quaint surroundings. So be severely disciplined to start with; imagination comes later.

That is why it is not necessarily easier to fit out a modern apartment than one dating from the last century or the beginning of this one. On the contrary, the typical town apartment was designed for a specific kind of life. Its floor plan was laid out in accordance with certain precise functions. Austere and conventional though that plan may appear to us today, it nevertheless has balance. A few modifications are all that is needed to lend it fresh charm and adapt it to the modern concept.

Exposure, view, and light are the next things to be taken into consideration. They constitute unalterable data: no subsequent second thoughts can correct mistakes made at this stage.

Finally, take care of the comfort element. And if this is inadequate or needs attention, whatever changes you have to make must not destroy the original architectural concept.

In fact before doing anything at all, make the following your inflexible principle in matters of interior design: "yes" to all improvements; "no" to anything that alters the character of the original.

Architects, interior designers

The architect expresses his client's needs and requirements in terms of plane and volume. He is responsible at the technical and aesthetic levels for all construction problems both outside and inside.

The interior designer's job, whether he is dealing with a new building—in which case he will work in close collaboration with the architect—or remodelling an old apartment, is to think out the floor plan of the dwelling, shape space in such a way as to get the most out of it, move or remove partition walls, assign functions, and distribute circulation areas. He is in fact the "town planner" of your interior.

On a smaller scale it is the interior designer's job to create an ambience. He chooses the furniture, materials, and colours; he disposes lines and mass, balancing occupied against unoccupied space; he arranges the lighting. In making these choices he must of course take account of his client's tastes and personality. If he does not, the home he creates will never be anything but a lifeless décor slapped onto an architectural structure.

It is important that the sensibilities of architect and interior designer be in tune with those of their client. Ultimately success depends as much upon this natural sympathy and upon mutual confidence as upon talent and material resources.

II

The floor plan

Space and function

It is not the number of rooms but the judicious distribution of space and allocation of function that make it possible to live more comfortably in one apartment than in another. A well laid-out five-room apartment is more pleasant to live in than a badly organized one with seven rooms.

In the case of the traditional apartment, the purpose of each room has to be rethought and brought more into line with modern life. A balance must be found between space, function, and degree of occupation. For example:

— A large living room with a section set aside for meals is preferable to a small drawing room plus separate dining room.
— The dining room, in use for only two hours of the day, can serve some other purpose as well.
— Library and study can be made into one.
— The corridor, an otherwise dead space, will come to life if put to some practical use.

A large living room with a section
set aside for meals is preferable to
a small drawing room plus separate
dining room.

— The entrance hall serves the principal rooms while preserving their independence.

The floor plan is governed by certain logical imperatives: the dining area, for example, will be near the kitchen; the sleeping quarters will be near the bathroom but as far as possible from areas of activity and circulation.

Division of space

A new floor plan involves some modification of the space set aside for each activity. Depending on the particular case, a number of solutions are possible:

— Moving and redistributing partition walls in accordance with the redistribution of areas.
— Using the Japanese system of sliding panels or roll-blinds to separate two functionally different parts of the same room when required.
— Suggesting a semi-partition or a separation by means of a piece of furniture (couch, bookshelf, long table, etc.).

Circulation axes

Room-to-room circulation must be fluid and relaxed, in contrast to that of the corridor serving the apartment as a whole. This is the principle of the suite of rooms in classical architecture, with communication along the façade wall.
Find a supple rhythm that does not seal off any of your spaces. A space enclosed is immediately a prison.
Work out a circular path between the different reception areas of a room and a number of adjoining rooms. On no account should visitors ever find themselves in a dead end and be forced to retrace their steps.

Use screens to separate two functionally different parts of the same room when required.

III

The principles of laying out a floor plan

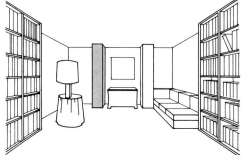

Conceal a load-bearing post or pillar by incorporating it in a row of pilasters.

Surfaces

Walls, floor, and ceiling determine the structure of a room. If that structure is un-balanced or otherwise ill-con-ceived, it is impossible to create a pleasant living space.

Take radical action at the start: lower a ceiling here, remove or add a partition wall there, alter a door or window. This will work out more cheaply than resorting afterwards to arbitrary remedies. Better now to employ the bricklayer than the cabinet-maker later.

Walls

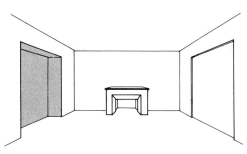

Balance an alcove lying at right angles to a dominant, axis-forming element in a room by creating a shallower alcove in the opposite wall.

A wall that is in the way can be removed either by replacing it with a transparent partition or by transforming it visually by means of colour (use of bright, shiny materials) or lighting effects, or by covering it with mirror.

In some apartments, the walls have projections or other architectural irregularities. Such accidents can often be turned to

A wall that is in the way can be
removed by transforming it visually
through the use of shiny materials.

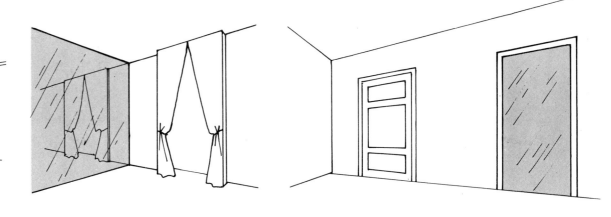

good effect either by frankly stressing them or by incorporating them in the décor. For example:

— An important element in a room—a fireplace, perhaps—sets up an axis. If the wall at right angles to that element contains an alcove, the room will lack balance. Restore harmony to the proportions by creating a shallower recess in the wall opposite the alcove.

— A load-bearing and consequently indispensable post or pillar can be "removed" visually by incorporating it in

a row of pilasters that set up a spatial rhythm.

— Projections and recesses offer a way of enlivening walls—for example by fitting bookshelves into them—and "building in" important pieces of furniture.

Structural irregularities can thus be turned into pretexts for decoration or axes of decorative interest.

Mirrors

Mirrors clearly have the power to create an illusion of space. They have played an important

part in interior design ever since the eighteenth century. By judicious use of mirrors you can multiply your effects:

— Covering a low ceiling with a mirror will double the scale of a room.

— A piece of wall may stick out awkwardly; a mirror on the projecting surface will make it less obtrusive.

— A mirror covering the wall at right angles to the window wall will double the proportions of a room as well as making it brighter by reflecting the view.

— A large mirror placed oppo-

Mirrors have the power to create an illusion of space.

By judicious use of mirrors you can multiply your effects.

Mirrors can trick the eye into fresh perspectives and break up the monotonous parallels of a narrow room.

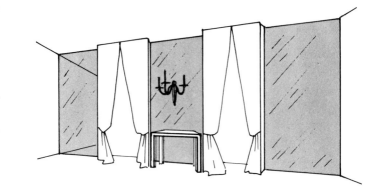

A mirror between a pair of windows or mirrors on either side of a window will increase your luminous area by giving the illusion of a single, broad bay.

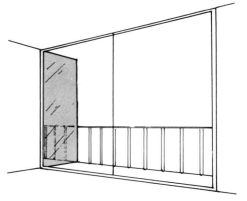

A mirror on the party wall of a balcony or terrace will double the depth of perspective.

A mirror in a window embrasure will make the window look larger; covering the wall below a window, it will give the illusion of a single bay reaching from floor to ceiling.

site a door will, by suggesting a suite of rooms, add depth to the perspective.

— A corner window or door robs a room of balance. A symmetrically placed mirror on the same wall will restore harmony.

— A mirror set in the embrasure of an opening or shallow recess will have an enlarging effect.

— Mirrors on the sides of a window embrasure will reflect the view *ad infinitum*, give better light distribution, and make the window seem larger than it is.

— A mirror on the wall below or above a window will give the illusion of a single bay reaching from floor to ceiling.

— A mirror between a pair of windows, or mirrors on either side of a window, will increase your luminous area by giving the illusion of a single, broad bay.

— A mirror on the party wall of a balcony or terrace will double the depth of perspective by reflecting the lateral view.

— A mirror in the back of a glass cabinet will show off the reverse side of a piece of sculpture, vase, or other exhibit.

— A half-moon bracket fixed to a wall mirror will suggest a pedestal table.

A large mirror placed opposite a door will, by suggesting a suite of rooms, add depth to the perspective.

A mirror covering the wall at right angles to the window wall will double the proportions of a room.

A mirror on the wall below a window will give the illusion of a single bay reaching from floor to ceiling.

Mirrors on the sides of a window embrasure will make the window seem larger than it is.

These are just a few visual tricks that will introduce fresh perspectives, break up the monotonous parallels of a narrow room, and lend charm to a mediocre piece of architecture.

Another trick of mirrors is that they constitute a supplementary light source, adding by reflection to the brightness of a room.

A mirror, however, can look very hard. One way of softening the surface is by placing something in front of it—a statue, for example, or a plant. You can even hang a painting or a wall clock on it as was done in the eighteenth century.

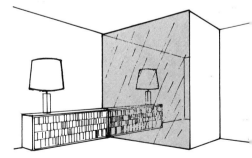

A piece of wall may stick out
awkwardly ; a mirror on the projecting surface will make it less
obtrusive.

21

The floor can be used to make space look larger, break it up, or otherwise modulate it.

Differences of level define different areas without interrupting either eye or movement.

Floors

The floor, too, like the walls, can be used to make space look larger, break it up, or otherwise modulate it.

Flooring of uniform texture or colour will create a link between two or more rooms with different functions: for example between hall and living room, study and drawing room, or drawing room and dining room. This kind of continuity between one room and another also creates an illusion of greater spaciousness. If the room is large enough, different areas can be distinguished by differences of level: for example between dining area and lounge area, or to mark off a conversation corner in the living room or the sleeping area in a bedroom. Differences of level define different areas without interrupting either eye or

If the room is large enough, different areas can be distinguished by differences of level.

movement. They suggest a relaxed, interesting ambience. To create such a difference of level, it is simpler to raise the floor than to lower it. With a normal 8′ 6″ (2.60 m) ceiling the floor can be raised to a height of 18″ (45 cm) (three steps). A dark floor gives a more solid foundation to a room and will merge with dark furniture of the same value if not of the same colour.

A light-coloured floor will set off dark furniture. The contrast must not be too sharp, however, or the furniture will give an impression of floating in space like flies in a jug of milk.

A number of factors will determine your choice of flooring: climate, the ambience and the function of the room, and the style in which it is furnished. Stone or marble flags give a suggestion of pomp and ceremony. On a more modest level, terracotta tiles go well in the country or in a warm climate. Wood and fitted wall-to-wall carpeting, on the other hand, being warm materials, are more suited to cold or temperate climates.

There is nothing like the latter for the impression of comfort, luxury, and intimacy that it lends to any dwelling. In a suite of rooms, use the same colour as much as possible: your apartment will look more spacious.

Patterned carpeting and tiling make it possible to create optical effects that will add interest to a long corridor, for example. You can heighten the effect by using the same pattern on the walls.

Carpets

A carpet or area rug is more than simply an element of decoration or comfort: it offers a further method of circumscribing in a neat way a particular functional area—for example a fireside corner, lounge corner,

You can heighten the optical effect by using the same pattern on walls and floor.

A rug offers a method of circumscribing in a neat way a particular functional area.

dining area, or circulation area. Choose in preference large carpets that will lend scale to a room. Avoid the "postage-stamp" kind, particularly laid at an angle. Their skimpiness will demean any décor. A figured carpet laid on a uniform floor adds a graphic, fanciful note that furniture cannot always give. Be careful to avoid any violent clash with the other elements in the room, however; the colour of your carpet must always be in tune with the ambience.

In a large living room a part of the ceiling can be lowered in order to create a cosier corner.

To lend intimacy to a high-ceilinged room, create a mezzanine, which will at the same time give you extra space.

Ceilings

A ceiling need not always present a uniform surface. There are various ways in which it can be used to heighten the ambience of a room:

— In an old house or apartment, the ceilings may be up to 13′ (4 m) high. In order to lend more intimacy to a room, rather than lowering the ceiling, which will destroy the harmony of the original proportions, it is better to create a mezzanine, which will at the same time give you extra space. Alternatively you can broaden the proportions by creating horizontals in the room, you can throw the lighting downwards and leave the ceiling in darkness, or you can even paint the ceiling in some dark colour or combination of colours.

— If a room is large enough—you can do this in a large living room, for example—a part of the ceiling can be lowered in order to create a cosier corner.

— If the ceiling of a room is too low, you can restore harmony

A ceiling can be used to heighten the ambience of a room.

Papering the ceiling identically with the walls will strengthen the decorative unity of a room.

If the ceiling of a room is too low, you can restore harmony to the proportions by decorating it with a brilliant gloss paint or even covering it with a mirror.

to the proportions by decorating it with a brilliant gloss paint or even covering it with a mirror.
— Narrow rooms (halls, corridors, bathrooms, etc.) will look wider if their ceilings are lowered.
— Painting the ceiling the same colour as the walls or covering it with the same wallpaper will strengthen the unity of a room, lend it intimacy, and create an all-round feeling of comfort.

The timbered ceiling is widely regarded as the acme of interior design—an idea that is overdue for correction. Genuine beams are primarily of structural importance. Their interest as a decorative element, though appreciable, is not sufficient to justify exposing them at all costs.
Rounded vaults in corridors and ridged ceilings in rooms lend added intimacy. They impart a kind of psychological comfort.

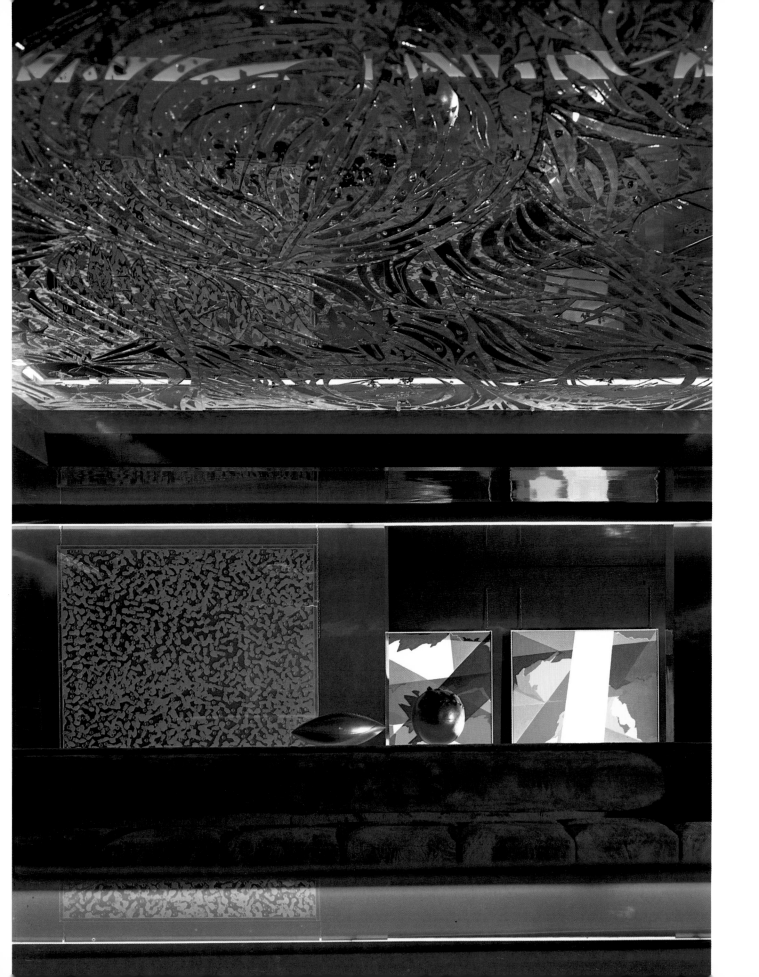

Avoid grouping your verticals on one side and your horizontals on the other.

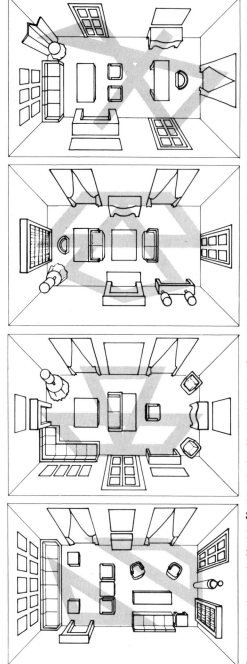

Lines

Doors, windows, pieces of furniture, and other decorative and architectural elements are defined by combinations of vertical and horizontal lines.

When designing a room, avoid grouping your verticals on one side and your horizontals on the other. Aim on the contrary for unity of line and mass; put rounded shapes with rounded shapes, straight lines with straight lines. (Identity of line is here more important than identity of period or place of origin.)

This unity, however, must never be allowed to give rise to monotony or boredom. Set up a high/low alternation, not systematically but in such a way as to engender a natural, living rhythm (think of a mountain range with its peaks, plateaux, and valleys). In doing so, take into account the levels of your seating, of which there are two: that of the seat proper (about 1′ 6″ [45 cm]) and that of the back (about 2′ 4″ [72 cm]), the latter corresponding to the height of a dresser, table, desk, etc.

Decorative and architectural elements are defined by combinations of vertical and horizontal lines.

Horizontal lines give an impression of relaxation and comfort. They go with a young, modern, uncomplicated life-style.

Set up a high/low alternation in such a way as to engender a natural, living rhythm.

Psychological effect:

This movement of lines is not only an aesthetic problem but also one of ambience:

— *Horizontal lines* give an impression of relaxation and comfort. They go with a young, modern, uncomplicated life-style.
— *Vertical lines* give an impression of dignity and pomp. They predominated in classical and ceremonial styles from the Middle Ages to the nineteenth century, and their place is in reception rooms.

— *Curved lines* give a feeling of well-being, inviting one to "let go." Much used in the eighteenth century, they are today coming back into their own in sinuous easy-chair designs that hug the lines of the body.

Masses

Whether it be an armchair, a table, a settee, or a bookshelf, every article of furniture is primarily a mass relating to other masses. As far as furniture is concerned, then, the collectivity takes precedence over the unit. An isolated piece of furniture has no more meaning than a musical note out of context.

Curved lines are coming back into their own today in sinuous easy-chair designs that echo living movements.

Each furnishing complex in a room corresponds to a particular function: relaxation, reading, work, play, eating, etc. Between these complexes there should be neutral areas providing visual ventilation as well as facilitating circulation. This kind of alternation of solids and spaces will structure your room space and avoid both the unaesthetic "hole" and a dull waiting room style of alignment of pieces of furniture around the walls.

If the room is a large one, furnish the centre. Provide a nucleus of peace, intelligently appointed, for moments of repose and privacy. Such an arrangement will give an impression of spaciousness: if you leave the walls free they will appear to recede. At all events, "bevel" the corners of your room by emphasizing a circular, enveloping movement between the various areas. A single element—statue, plant, corner-cupboard, screen—is all that is needed.

A large piece of furniture set at right angles or at an acute angle to the wall can affect a room in one or more of a number of similar ways. (We are speaking of a deliberate arrangement, of course, and not of the unfortunate propensity of cleaning women to leave things askew!)

Every article of furniture is primarily a mass relating to other masses. As far as furniture is concerned, the collectivity takes precedence over the unit.

A large piece of furniture may proportionally increase the scale of a small room.

A large piece placed centrally against a wall will impose a certain discipline on a room. Placed off-centre, it will entail a subtler, less rigorous composition. It may be balanced by an equivalent but not necessarily equal mass. For example:

— a desk by a console-table plus a bronze statuette or a picture;
— a screen by a pedestal table plus a lamp.

In principle, avoid having two pieces of equal size side by side against the same wall. This kind of arrangement is possible, however, when the two are separated by an intermediate element—a chimney-piece between two sets of bookshelves, for example—

where the effect derives from symmetry.

The answer to the question of whether a piece of furniture should be on the same scale as the room it is placed in is: generally speaking, yes. Imagine the delicate curves of an eighteenth-century chair beneath the majestic vaults of a mediaeval castle. Its gracefulness would be made to seem affected.

If the room is a large one, furnish the centre.

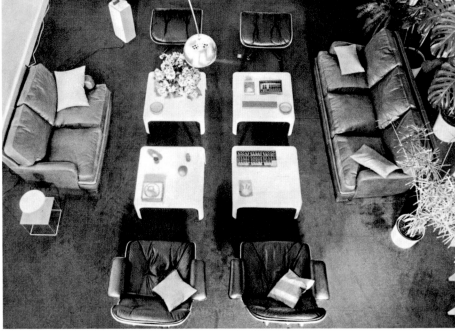

There are, however, exceptions to this rule: for example, a large piece of furniture may in certain cases proportionally increase the scale of a small room. The same may apply the other way round if the architectural elements (fireplace, door, etc.) are very much under the normal size.

One way of either sharpening or blurring the definition of a mass is through colour. Violent colours will make it stand out; neutral or ambient colours will soften its outline and make it merge into the background.

IV Architectural elements

Pillars and beams

As load-bearing elements, pillars and beams form part of the structure of a room. It may prove desirable to turn their possibly awkward presence to advantage by drawing them into the décor and making them an integral part of it. For example:

— Structural elements can be made to define a particular area of activity or serve as point of departure for a movable partition or a bookshelf.
— Surrounded by plants or used as a background to set off a piece of sculpture, a pillar can become an axis of your décor.
— Painted or papered like the wall, it provides a place to hang prints or *objets d'art*.

Finally, remember what the great French architect Auguste Perret said: "The man who conceals a beam is making a mistake. The man who makes a false beam is committing a crime."

Turn an awkward pillar to advantage by using it as point of departure for a bookshelf.

A pillar can become an axis of your décor.

A fireplace is first and foremost
a setting for a fire.

The setting should be simple and without superfluous decoration, and its proportions must be in harmony with those of the room.

Fireplaces

Whether ancient or modern, rural or urban in style, a fireplace is first and foremost a setting for that primordial element—fire. There is nothing more cheering to eye and heart than a really good blaze.

In order not to detract from the fire's living presence, then, the setting should be simple—a hole in the wall—, without superfluous decoration. Never use more than two materials for a fireplace.

Make sure, too, that the proportions of the aperture are in harmony with those of the room. If it is too small it will look niggardly. A rectangular fireplace will fit well in a décor based on low horizontals.

Radiators

If the positioning of your radiators is unsatisfactory from the aesthetic point of view, have no hesitation in redistributing them. Ways of dealing with radiators are either to hide them or to highlight their presence.

Never use a radiator hood in the middle of a wall. This dreadful invention has the effect of turning the radiator into a piece of furniture, which will inevitably become cluttered with lamps, flowers, and other objects. The best solution is to incorporate the radiator in the structure of the room—niche, window recess—or build it into a bookshelf, for example. The front can be concealed with a metal or wooden screen in a colour that matches its surroundings.

An exposed radiator can be painted either like the wall or in a contrasting colour, in which case it will stand out like some enigmatic presence, assuming a pleasing, graphic quality. Nowadays you can get steel radiators in which function, design, and material are woven into a genuinely decorative whole.

Pipes

Camouflage is of course the most aesthetic solution, especially in reception rooms. In some cases, however, a possible alternative is frank acceptance, for example when a particular area of activity (playroom, lounge, toilets) is assigned to a cellar or somewhere where pipes and conduits are so obtrusive as to be difficult to conceal.

A simple hole in the
wall detracts least
from the fire's living
presence.

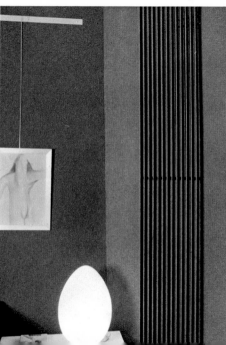

An exposed radiator can be made
to stand out against a wall with
a pleasing, graphic quality.

Windows

The function of the window is twofold:

— As regards form, it is part of the architecture; as regards décor, it is an integral part of the way in which the room as a whole is arranged.
The normal window poses no problems. As soon as a window is too tall, however, or too wide, or set at an angle, it becomes an obstacle to a balanced interior. This is where mirrors can be brought into play—to correct this kind of fault.

— It forms a link between exterior and interior space. A panoramic window covering the entire surface of a wall offers a way of marrying countryside and décor. Even when the view is exceptional, however, it is sometimes necessary to do as the Japanese do and break up the glass area rhythmically by means of rest areas for the eye. This can be done with:

— horizontal or vertical Venetian blinds;
— fabric blinds that unfold or unroll to different heights;
— interior shutters;
— curtains and casements for ordinary windows.

A panoramic window covering the
entire surface of a wall offers a way
of marrying countryside and décor.

It is sometimes
necessary to break
up a glass area
rhythmically by
means of rest areas
for the eye.

Horizontal or vertical Venetian blinds.

In the latter case, casement curtains which draw back take the place of fixed sheer curtains (useless when you have a beautiful view). Choose a translucent silk in a pastel or neutral shade to create a luminous ambience in the room. Closed at night, these casements will:

— shut out the darkness of the outside;

— create an alternation of materials and colours, thus avoiding of having the lined curtains draw across the whole width of the window.

By day, a curtain fixed permanently in front of a large window gives the illusion of a wall without the rigidity. There is nothing wrong with placing a piece of furniture against it or hanging a picture or mirror in

Blinds that unfold or unroll to different heights.

Interior shutters.

front of it in order to heighten the effect.

A table or a piece of sculpture, for example, placed in front of a window and viewed against the light, will be invested with a quality of heightened definition. It will also break the monotony of a uniform surface.

With a panoramic window of modern proportions, avoid any kind of classical sham: valances, swags, tie-backs, and so on.

Doors are an integral part of interior design. A large single door is less stately than a double door but just as effective.

A fine *objet d'art* placed in front of
a window and viewed against the
light will be invested with a quality
of heightened definition.

Doors

Doors, a vital aspect of interior design, are subject to the same laws as any other design element. There is a marked difference between the stately double door, reserved for reception rooms and still very much a feature of French interior design, and the single door. The former is not only wider than the latter; it must also be appreciably higher as is not the case in apartments of recent construction. Maximum and minimum dimensions for doors are as follows:

— single-leaf: between 2′ 4″ (70 cm) and 3′ 4″ (1 m) wide and 6′ 8″ (2 m) and 7′ 4″ (2.20 m) high;
— double-leaf: between 4′ 4″ (1.30 m) and 6′ 8″ (2 m) wide and 8′ (2.40 m) and 10′ (3 m) high.

Nowadays, then, a double door should reach right up to the ceiling, since in modern architecture this is rarely higher than 10′ (3 m). If it does not, what can be done to play down the resultant lack of proportion?

A good way is to use some such visual artifice as placing a picture above the door, or a wooden panel with a moulding to match the door, or extending the door jambs upwards, etc.
The more practical English solution has been to adopt a single door with a wide (3′ 4″ [1 m]) leaf. The result is less imposing but just as effective for reception purposes.

To be avoided are:

— *Sham doors*, as used on the pretext of restoring a fictitious balance.
— *Wallpapered doors:* they wear badly (stains and finger-prints show up on them, exposing the deception). Also, a room without visible doors gives a claustrophobic impression.
— *Doors that pretend to be bookshelves or sections of panelling:* just as a spade is a spade, so ought a door to be a door; eschew the false when decorating it. To cheat is to lose face with the knowledgeable.

The library

From one's childhood onwards, the library, whether at school or at home, is the den *par excellence*, the welcoming cocoon into which, surrounded by books, one can escape into one's dreams…
It must above all be a quiet room if it is to foster an atmosphere conducive to reading, whether for study or recreation.
The library as it used to be in every noble abode, lined with

By alternating groups of books and pieces of sculpture or *objets d'art* **you can create subtle centres of interest.**

The end arrangement will be a virtual portrait of its owner.

gleaming bindings behind glass or grilles, is tending to disappear, being rather too solemn and austere for our day and age. Nowadays we prefer to keep our books possibly in a special room or, failing this, in a part of the living room, in the hall, or in a corridor.

Moreover bookcases and bookshelves are extremely decorative. Modern books with their brightly coloured jackets and cloth bindings can add life and gaiety to any décor. And by alternating groups of books and pieces of sculpture or *objets*

d'art on the shelves you can create subtle centres of interest. Leaving room for the latter will give your bookshelves a less dense appearance and your books breathing-space. Pictures and photographs can also find a place in your bookshelves. Here anything goes, really, provided that it stems from some genuine aspiration and not from purely decorative motives. For the end arrangement will be a virtual portrait of its owner.
Lastly, your audio-visual equipment—record player, radio, loud speakers, tape recorder, television—will fit

naturally into the context of your books. It is a logical association.

Structurally a bookcase can be classical and deliberate (natural or painted wood) or it can be modern and seek to be invisible by being as light as possible (metal, glass, or Plexiglass construction).

A horizontal composition will restore balanced proportions to a high room. You can emphasize the horizontality of a bookcase by making the uprights very thin and bringing the shelves forward beyond them.

In a small room, the "plinth" effect—i.e., the table-high bookcase—will avoid any feeling of bookshelves bearing down on one.

Covering an entire wall from floor to ceiling with bookcases offers a way of modifying the architecture of a room by fram-

Leaving room for *objets d'art* **will give your bookshelves a less dense appearance and your books breathing-space.**

A row of spots set into the ceiling with their beams sweep down over the book bindings.

Record player, radio and tape recorder will fit naturally into the context of your books.

ing certain elements—fireplace, niche, door, or other aperture. Placed crosswise in a large room, a bookcase can be used to separate two distinct functional areas.

Shelves wide enough to take two rows of books (1′ 2″ [35 cm] to 1′ 6″ [40 cm]) should be fitted with a structure to raise the back row above the front, making it easier to get at.

Lighting plays an important part in setting off the books and objects on your shelves. Choose either:

— special shelf lamps that fit on the front edge of the shelf and have a metal "mask" that, if painted the same colour as the shelves, is invisible;
— a row of spots set into the ceiling with their beams sweeping down over the book bindings.

Covering an entire wall from floor to ceiling with bookcases offers a way of modifying the architecture of a room.

Special shelf lamps can be fitted on the front edge of the shelves. Their metal "mask" is invisible.

Light sources

Make it a golden rule to have a lot of different, low-wattage light sources.

Avoid "black holes", because they make a room look gloomy, and violent contrasts, because they are tiring to the eye. This is not of course to rule out a certain play of light and shadow that lends interest to space without chopping it up.

Do not light the ceiling. If necessary, shade any bulbs that throw light upwards. The room will gain in intimacy what it loses in brightness.

Chandelier or no chandelier? Yes, if... If the room is a very large one, if it is centralized, and if the ceiling is high enough (you must be able to walk underneath the chandelier without banging your forehead). But regard it as a luminous object rather than as a light source.

Have a lot of different, low-wattage light sources.

Suspended lamps permit the illumination of a specific area: dining table, game table, etc. The principle is admissible if

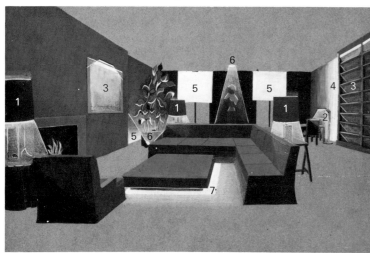

employed at least twice in the room and in such a way as to balance.

Then there is the problem of the lampshade: should it be translucent or opaque, white or coloured? Your choice will be dictated by the decorative effect required:

— A slightly tinted *translucent* shade—of natural silk or paper, beige, pink, or white lined with pink—will cast a glow that is warm without being actually coloured.
— *Opaque* shades cast an indirect light, part of it directed at the floor and part at the ceiling (the latter to be prevented by additional screening). If the shade is lined in a gold colour the light will be warm and welcoming. Silver and steel have a metallic coldness that is much less agreeable.

As a rule use only incandescent frosted-glass bulbs. Fluorescent lighting, suitably softened with a filter, may be used for glass cabinets, shelves, and niches—

with the tubes well concealed. A device that is coming more and more into use it the rheostat, which gives you complete control over the intensity of your lighting for every occasion. For the beginning of a party, for example, or before dinner, you want brilliant lighting; after the meal, towards the end of the evening, it needs to be softer. This kind of modulation superbly complements the psychological evolution of mood characteristic of a gathering of friends.

Concealed and visible light sources should be about equal in number.
From time to time, place special emphasis on decorative elements by the use of a spotlight. For example:

— Conceal a small spot behind a plant, for instance, to throw huge, mysterious shadows on wall or ceiling as required.
— A picture, piece of sculpture, or *objet d'art* can be effectively

**Concealed and visible light sources
should be about equal in number.**

Light a glass cabinet by means of horizontal strips concealed in the shelves.

A certain play of light and shadow can lend interest to space without chopping it up.

set off with a cluster of spots or a strip light.

Too much contrast, however, will make your picture look like a slide projection. Avoid any excessively theatrical effect by placing a lamp beside the piece you are illuminating; this will tone down the contrast and give the arrangement a more natural look. A room for living in is not a stage.

More generally, your living-room lighting must be adapted to the room's various functions:
— *festive* lighting for parties;
— *soft* lighting for more intimate occasions;
— *localized* lighting for each centre of interest;
— *secondary* lighting by concealed spots (setting off a particular decorative element: glass cabinet, work of art, plant, etc.).

An inside wall can be flood-lit like a façade.

For reading, writing, and playing cards put on general "mood" lighting plus direct lighting.

Light each area to suit its
function:

— Quiet corner for conversation:
Soft, reflected lighting. Think of
a woman's face: hard shadows
etch lines. Be careful, though:
light reflected by a coloured
surface (walls, curtains) under-
goes a change. Light only pale,
neutral tones—pink, beige,
ivory—that will diffuse a
flattering glow. Avoid to light
green, which makes people look
ill, blue, which makes them look
like corpses, and yellow, which
will give all your guests jaundice!
Decide on a lighting level and
put all the light sources at that
height (measuring the distance
from the floor to the middle of
the shade).

— For reading, writing, playing
cards, etc.:
General "mood" lighting, plus
direct lighting.

— Television corner:
Discreet ambient lighting to tone
down the brightness of the
screen and reduce a contrast that
is tiring to the eyes. A small
lamp that can be switched on and
off is useful for changing
channels, etc.

An inside wall can be flood-lit
in the same ways as a façade:

— by means of a vertical floor-
to-ceiling strip light or row of
spots concealed behind a tall
piece of furniture, pillar, or angle
in the wall. The light will be
bright near the source and shade
off gradually away from it;
— by means of a horizontal
arrangement of light sources at
floor or baseboard level;
— by means of a horizontal
arrangement running along the
ceiling, concealed behind a
valence. This is a good way of
lighting curtains, a mirror, or a
hanging.

Materials

VI

**Put your most costly material
where it can be seen and touched.**

Every décor will comprise a certain number of warm materials (wood, textiles, leather, fur) and a certain number of cold materials (marble, metal, glass, plastic). These materials may in turn be rough or smooth, shiny or matt, hard or soft.

As a general rule, avoid having more than three materials in a room. Use contrast, for example: rough walls/silky curtains and wallpapers; wooden furniture/glass or marble table-top. Putting different materials side by side will bring out their individuality. This is an important point to remember. Above all, avoid all pastiche materials: plastic made to look like wood, concrete cast like stone, and all the pretences that, in the context of a home, constitute a heresy.

Put your most costly material where it can be seen and touched: for example, chairs covered in silk velours in a room hung with linen (matt/shiny combination). This kind of contrast will give an impression of more refined luxury than will a profusion of expensive materials.

Every décor will comprise a certain number of warm and cold and a certain number of rough and smooth materials.

Putting different materials side by side will bring out their individuality.

Colour

VII

A colour scheme should unfold
like a musical composition.
It must have an underlying key,
and use a particular scale and
rhythm. The choice of colours—
like the choice of chords—and
the way they are placed together
will determine their style. There
are a number of ways of giving
a room harmony:

— *Black and white:*
Everything—walls, floor, ceiling,
curtains, upholstery—is either
black or white. The only
animation is in the variety of
materials.
All you need to make such a
room "sing" is a keynote: a
picture, a chair, cushions, a
flower arrangement. Another
way of creating an effect of
colour is by reflection off some
object onto a white surface.

— *Monochrome:*
This scheme is a harmonious
arrangement of graduated shades
of one colour—pale blue/
bright blue/navy, for example, or
raw silk/beige/brown.
A monochrome scheme will make

Everything is either black or white. All you need to make the room "sing" is a keynote.

Base your colour scheme on a major element in the décor—a picture or a carpet.

A monochrome scheme will make a room look larger and more interesting as well as give it distinction.

A monochrome colour scheme works with graduated shades of one colour.

a room look larger and more interesting as well as give it distinction and harmonize elements of different styles. A neutral shade on a wall—grey or sepia—will set off pictures and *objets d'art* to advantage, playing, as it were, a discreet accompaniment.

— *Polychrome:*
This kind of scheme admits combinations of colours that are related (yellow/red/orange), complementary (blue/red, yellow/purple), or contrasting (white/brown/orange, red/black/white). It needs to be used with skill and in moderation if it is to avoid the pitfall of vulgarity. The surest guide to polychrome harmony is a good painting (usually a good reproduction will do). Study the work as a whole and the way the colours relate to one another. Work out how much of the painted area each colour takes up: blue 40%, green 10%, red 5%, for example. Notice how these colours are distributed: a painter will never put two powerful

colours side by side because they would cancel each other out. Try to achieve the same balance and the same proportional distribution of the colours in your room.
Another approach that can be effective is to base your colour scheme on a major element in the décor: a picture, a carpet, or a hanging. Pick out the dominant colours—not more than three, though!—and echo them in your wallpaper, curtains, chaircovers and cushions.

Beware of fashionable colours:

— they soon start to get on your nerves;
— they go out of fashion;
— they do not necessarily fit into a given décor.

A sacrifice to the taste of the moment, however, is sometimes a great temptation. Resist it as far as large surfaces and basic elements are concerned; give in when it is a question of details that can be easily replaced (cushions, objects, and so on).

The surest guide to polychrome harmony is a good painting.

A polychrome scheme admits combinations of related colours.

VIII

Audio-visual appliances

Where should you put your television set? Never build it into or stand it in the principal corner of the living room. It will drive out any kind of social life; people will watch it and conversation will come to a standstill. This is the mistake most commonly made when installing a corner for conversation.
The television corner should be autonomous and at some distance from all other activities so that people can use it without being disturbed and without disturbing those who do not want to look at it. The ideal solution is of course a separate, small room specially fitted out for television. Among other things this will obviate family squabbles about programmes. Never camouflage a television set on the grounds that as a modern, functional appliance it is anachronistic in certain décors. The result is always hideous. Even framed in a set of shelves, it loses the flexibility that is so much a part of it. It is better to accept it frankly as a modern piece of furniture that, if well conceived and designed, will go with any décor.

The same applies to record players, film projectors, and so on. The increasingly sophisticated design of such appliances means that they can hold their aesthetic own in the best company.
After all, we find nothing shocking about a Rover parked outside Lincoln Cathedral.

The ideal solution is to put the television in a separate, small room specially fitted out for viewing.

The increasingly sophisticated design of audio-visual appliances means that they can hold their aesthetic own in the best company.

Better to accept audio-visual appliances frankly as modern pieces of furniture that will go with any décor.

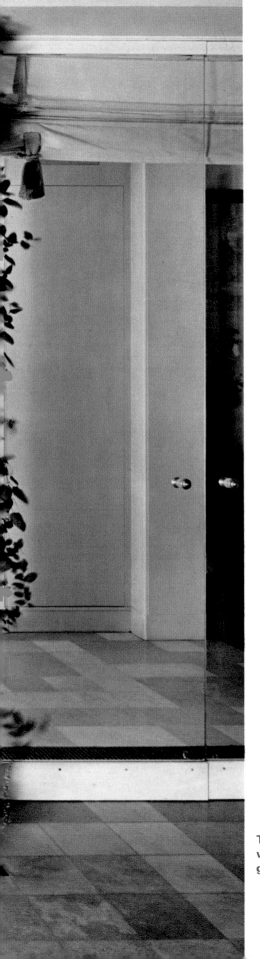

The hall is to a house
what the curtain
going up is to a stage.

Part Two

IX

Hall and corridors

The hall is to a house what the curtain going up is to a stage: it introduces the visitor to the atmosphere of a home. It has a psychological role and must play it with tact and verve. Avoid above all that cold, anonymous, strictly functional look that is so depressing. Admit an element of exuberance, even of extravagance, something that will capture people's attention, sharpen their senses, and put them in the mood for contact. As a place where guests are welcomed but which they pass quickly through, the hall can be allowed to overstate your personality slightly in order to establish your "image," as it were.

Plan

The logical thing is for the hall to serve the principal rooms, especially the living room. The link between hall and living

Admit an element of exuberance, even of extravagance.

room is generally established through colour, with the former presaging the latter in a higher key.

The best solution, when the structure of the premises and the occupants' life-style make it possible, is to have no door between hall and living room. This will give you more space, open things up, and make it easier to move about.

Furniture

A spacious, well-arranged hall can complement one or more of the rooms leading off it: a corner with comfortable chairs makes a useful extension of the living room, convenient for a tête-à-tête; put a bookshelf in the hall and you can display books and *objets d'art* there. Details like these will provide a foretaste of the warmth and intimacy of the rest of the house, making people feel at home the minute they step inside.

Do not forget the utilitarian aspect: a table where people can deposit whatever they have in their hands when they come in (handbag, gloves, mail, parcels, etc.); a mirror, preferably full-length, for your female guests; and of course somewhere for people to put their hats and coats—a clothes rack at the very least, and possibly a separate dressing room.

Doors

Finely proportioned, moulded or carved doors are an integral part of all interior design.

A door can also be combined with a large mirror to add depth to a room and suggest a mysterious perspective. But avoid glass doors, whether transparent or opaque, that diffuse light from another source. They are an aberration.

The many doors that lack any ornamental character—cupboard doors, service doors, etc.—must be treated with discretion: either paint them the same colour as the wall or conceal them with some kind of hanging or *portière*. This is the only instance where a *portière* offers an acceptable way of hiding an "unwanted" door. Besides camouflaging, it insulates—particularly against noise—and adds to the intimacy of the interior.

Lighting

Your light source should be either natural or artificial, never half-and-half. Combine:

—*ambient* lighting to bring out the pattern of parquet floor, carpet, or tiling;
— *localized* lighting—a lamp at elbow height—to add greater intimacy.

And for a dramatic touch:

— a spot directed onto a piece of sculpture or other object;
— a strip light above a picture that reflects the light;
— strip lights concealed along the edges of shelves to set off books and objects placed on them.

The hall, together with the corridor and the dining room, is one of the places where decorative effects can safely be taken a long way.

The hall can be allowed to overstate your personality slightly.

A corner with comfortable chairs and a full-length mirror provide a foretaste of the warmth and intimacy of the home.

Corridors

Every corridor is so much dead space and can in most cases be done away with as such, and be lined with closets. This kind of arrangement avoids the monotony of the traditional corridor, leaves room for such practical features as wardrobes, cupboards, a telephone corner, etc., and still preserves the independence of the areas served.

If for architectural reasons the corridor has to be retained, there are various ways of improving its appearance:

— *Using special materials:* a shiny surface—varnish, metal, laminated plastic—will pick up reflections and create an illusion of space.

— *Using colour:* paint walls and ceiling the same colour or paper them uniformly, with the doors standing out in contrast.

— *Using lighting:* clusters of spots distributed alternately along the two walls will set up a rhythm of lighted areas and shadows that will break the monotony of the perspective. A similar effect can be obtained with a lighted ceiling: alternating lateral strips of light and shadow will, by creating masses, add life and interest.

— *By lowering the ceiling or vaulting it:* stress a difference in height from the other rooms. In recovering a certain autonomy the corridor will become more interesting.

— *By modifying its function:*

hang pictures in it, or use it to display a collection, for example on wall-brackets, or, if it is wide enough, put in a bookshelf to hold a mixture of books and *objets d'art.*

In such ways a corridor will cease to be a cold, dead place and become an integral part of the life and charm of the dwelling.

A large mirror adds depth to a room
and suggests a mysterious
perspective.

X Drawing room, living room

The two terms cover a single reality: a room in which one can relax, receive guests, enjoy oneself, and generally slip into the context of the home without bothering anyone else. In fact a " space for living in," fitted out with a maximum of tact and affording a maximum of comfort and pleasure.

Depending upon the occupants' life-style, this room will be more or less luxurious, hinged to a greater or lesser extent on this or that aspect of social or family life or personal activities and

A " space for living in ", fitted out with a maximum of tact and affording a maximum of comfort and pleasure.

tastes. But the prime objective today is intimacy rather than pomp.

The important thing, regardless of style, furnishing, or colour scheme, is that one should feel at home in it, at any hour of the day or night, whether alone or with friends.

This kind of practical comfort comes before aesthetic comfort. Before you think "décor," then, think in terms of structure, i.e., of surface, mass, and line. For a harmonious body you must have a well constructed skeleton.

And remember: the broad lines that govern the arrangement of your living room—the heart of your house as it were—can be applied to the other rooms as well.

The different areas

Fireplaces, windows, and large doors constitute magnetic poles, drawing the eye to a fine blaze, out into the landscape, etc. It is around them that the life of the room will naturally organize itself. Draw up a plan, noting their positions and marking in the main axes of symmetry and the axes of circulation.

The different living areas should figure on your plan as circles of various diameters (paper discs will help you to decide your layout). Put the largest circle near the main centre of attraction—either facing it or at an angle, depending on the arrangement. Then distribute the smaller circles, leaving spaces between them for circulation.

Avoid having areas of equal importance. Even if your room comprises only two, one of them must predominate.

Allot to each area its function: relaxation, reception, reading, games, music, television, and possibly study and dining as

The different living areas should figure on your plan as circles of various diameters. Put the largest circle near the main centre of attraction.

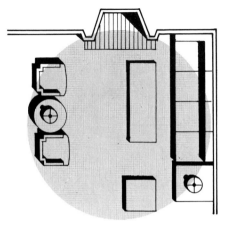
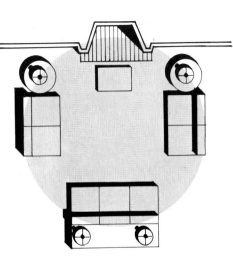
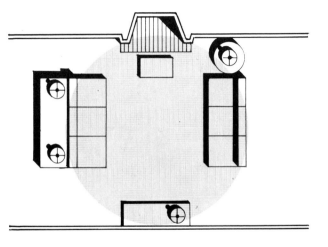

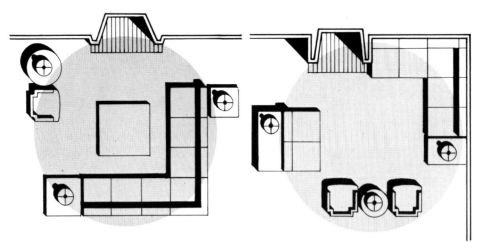

The maximum diameter for cosy conversation is 13' (4 m).

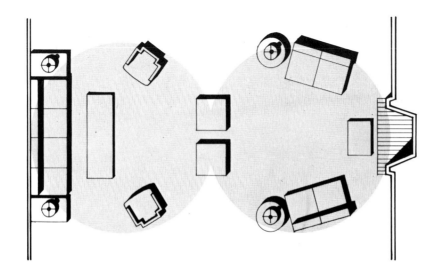

well. If your room is not very large it is better to pair compatible functions in the same area, e.g., relaxation/reception, games/dining, music/television, etc. Otherwise you will have congestion and chaos.

Distinguish the different areas by means of:

— a rug that contrasts with your wall-to-wall carpeting, parquet, or tile flooring. A rug draws together the components of a circle and stresses their unity. It must, however, be large enough to pass under the seats. Otherwise it will give a skimpy, cramped impression;

— a difference of level, whether up onto a podium or down into a well;

— a piece of furniture (bookshelf or long table) placed at an angle to suggest a partition.

Conversation corner

This is the village green, the meeting place of the room. It is the nucleus of hospitality, the home within a home.

Fireplace and windows constitute magnetic poles. It is around them that the life of the room will naturally organize itself.

The conversation area is the village green, the meeting place of the room. It is the nucleus of hospitality, the home within a home.

Things to remember:

— The maximum diameter here is 13′ (4 m). Beyond that conversation becomes impossible.
— No axis of circulation must be allowed to intersect this circle. Avoid a door by the fireplace. If necessary use screens to deflect movement around the outside of the circle and strengthen the feeling of well-being and security within it. This isolation is relative, however; you must avoid creating a "world unto itself." Life goes on moving among the different areas. Guests may form groups but not ignore or turn their backs on one another. Independence within interdependence—the very principle of courtesy.

**Furnishing is a matter of family
or social requirements.**

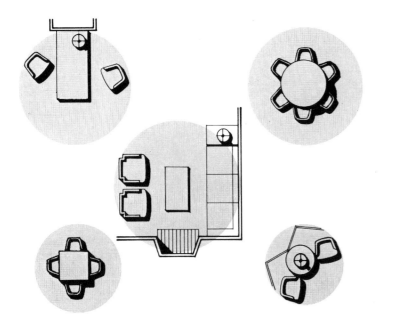

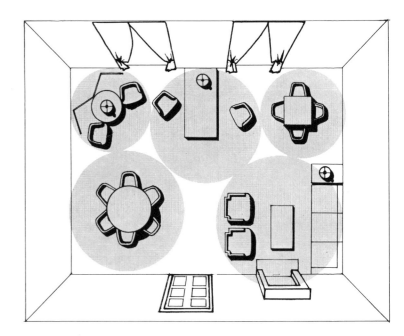

Furniture

Depending upon family or social requirements you will have:

— one or two sofas;
— two or three easy chairs chosen as much for comfort as for looks.

Their arrangement will vary according to circumstances— i.e., whether the settees are placed facing one another, at right angles, in a sunken "conversation well," etc.

Remember your accessories:

— *good lighting* to read by;
— *a fairly wide*, *low table* to put cigarettes and coffee cups on, hold an ashtray, and generally relieve people of whatever they may have in their hands and want to get rid of;
— *a bookshelf* or *magazine rack* to hold books, newspapers, and magazines tidily and yet within easy reach.

Circulation axes

Avoid as far as possible any direct links between different areas. Think instead of the winding paths of a country-house garden, threading their way through romantic coppices. This kind of movement will create an illusion of space, continually presenting, as one moves round this or that piece of furniture, some fresh aspect of the décor to the eye. Circulation in a living room must be fluid and easy so that your guests, even when there are a lot of them, can always move about freely.

Never block access to the windows, which incidentally must be easy to open at all times. Make it a golden rule that an axis of circulation must provide access to an area without ever encroaching on the area itself.

The arrangement of the furniture
will vary according to circumstances,
i.e., whether the settees are placed
facing one another, at right
angles, or in a well.

A rug that contrasts with your fitted
carpeting will draw together the
components of a circle.

XI Dining room, dining area

Dine seated or lounging, according to mood.

Modern taste prefers to dine at small tables.

The dining room as traditionally conceived has had its day. It has ceased to be a lifeless room used only at mealtimes to become a room in its own right with other functions to fill between meals. Depending upon size and floor plan, it will constitute an extension of living room, library, or study, or a small, separate reception room for intimate parties. It has been drawn into the rhythm of the dwelling as a whole.

The table is no longer the centre of everything but a mere accessory. It can be placed in a corner or along or at right angles to the wall. For a party it can be removed altogether. The full-scale ceremonial banquet with damask tablecloth is out today. Modern taste prefers buffet-style parties with small tables of be-

A meal is a festive occasion and everything should contribute towards making it as brilliant as possible.

tween four and six guests. Contacts are made more quickly, people form groups by affinity, and if you like they can even serve themselves. The folding tables (card tables) used on such occasions can be removed when the meal is over.

Dining nomad-fashion

Are we perhaps going back to our roots here? Up until the eighteenth century customs were still influenced by the nomadic life our ancestors used to lead. The table, a simple board laid on trestles, was set up anywhere —antechamber, bedchamber, cabinet, or great hall. The joyful atmosphere of these impromptu meals is splendidly captured in the work of the seventeenth-century French engraver Abraham Bosse. Royalty picnicked in the fields or dined informally in a private room with a few select friends. Why should we not resume the old custom, throw off the out-worn conventions of the nine-teenth century, and dine in all freedom according to mood, the season, and our guests in the garden, on the terrace, around the fire, in a winter garden, or even in a spacious entrance hall?

An exotic touch

And why not take advantage of today's predilection for foreign travel by dining in an exotic setting—on a low table, Japanese-style, or with cushions and a tray, as if one were in Morocco or India? Moreover the setting can be a pretext for serving exotic dishes. Your guests will appreciate the invitation to "get away from it all."

A meal is a festive occasion and everything should contribute towards making it as brilliant as possible. Have no hesitation in overdecorating a prosaically traditional room. Curious pictures and objects, aggressive colour schemes, mirrors— everything that would seem superfluous and tiring to the eye in the drawing room can be brought into play here. In centuries gone by the Mongol khans used to dazzle their visitors with their sumptuous halls lined with concave mirrors that multiplied the candle flames to infinity.

Eating in the living room

The ideal position for a dining table in the living room is:

— by a window, because it is pleasant to lunch by daylight;
— away from any axes of circulation and handy for the kitchen.

This arrangement, however, should only be used if your floor plan gives you no alternative. The fact that your guests see a ready-laid table when they arrive and have the unedifying spectacle of piles of debris when the meal is over does indeed constitute a major disadvantage. So if you are obliged to adopt this solution, try to shut off the table from the rest of the room by means of a screen.

An exotic touch carries an invitation to "get away from it all."

Customs were influenced by the nomadic life.

The dining room can constitute an extension of the kitchen.

Eating in the kitchen offers an excellent pretext for giving charm and life to a functional room.

Eating in the kitchen

This practical solution, which in addition offers an excellent pretext for giving charm and life to a functional room, can cover a variety of uses:
— servants' meals;

— children's breakfasts and after-school snacks;
— quick snacks over the weekend, or even small informal suppers after the theatre.

Dine in a winter garden if you feel like it.

Lighting for the dining room

The table can be lit from the ceiling (apart from the hall, this is the only place where this is permissible) by means of:

— a chandelier or other lamp hanging very low;
— spots sunk in the ceiling (movable spots will make it possible to concentrate the light on the table);
— a movable standard lamp with a telescopic arm (useful if the table is not always in the same place). This is the kind of lighting used for game tables.

With rheostat switches you will be able to vary the intensity of your lighting: a muted effect for informal occasions; in other circumstances, brighter.

Back up your direct lighting with ambient lighting or localized lighting for dramatic effect: lamps placed on pieces of furniture, spots concealed behind plants or directed on a picture or other object.

And do not forget to have candles. The soft, flickering light of candles is flattering to the female complexion—a point not to be overlooked!
Choose tall candlesticks for preference that will not get in the way of guests sitting opposite one another. The flames should never be at eye-level but always a little above.
Small, painted metal shades, nineteenth-century style, go well with period candlesticks. They cast a more mysterious light than do translucent shades, without colouring the light in a way that might not flatter your guests' faces nor go with the food they are eating.

Curious pictures and objects as well as mirrors can be brought into play here.

Spots sunk in the ceiling make it possible to concentrate light on the table.

XII

The bedroom

The bedroom has a splendid history, of course, particularly in France (from the stately bedchambers of the seventeenth century to the boudoirs of Proust's heroines) where it once constituted the hub of social life, indeed of life as a whole. But there is another tradition too—that of the bedroom as a haven of peace, of relaxation. The goal of the modern bedroom is simply this: to provide the best possible environment for those essential hours of calm and rest.

Plan

The bedroom should be in the vicinity of bathroom and toilet and at a distance from areas of activity, hospitality, and traffic. An increasingly popular solution is to have bedroom and bathroom form a single unit, with only a suggestion of a division between them rather than an arbitrary separation—a luxurious version of the ancient myth of man living and sleeping by a spring, fount of all life.

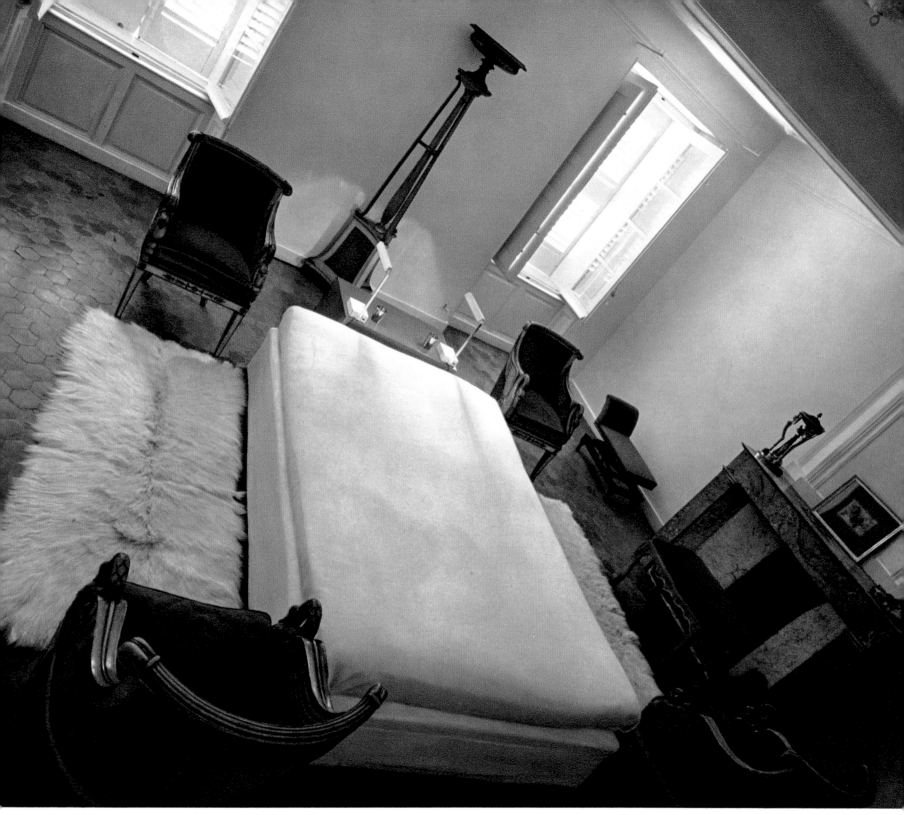

The centrepiece of the bedroom
is the bed. It may literally occupy
the middle of the room.

Furniture

Keep this strictly to a minimum:
— One or two beds. The bed is the centrepiece of the room and no pains should be spared to make it as comfortable as possible, even if it consists of no more than a mattress placed on a dais. The way the bed faces will depend on the occupant; some people can only sleep with their heads to the north, others with their heads to the south.
— Two bedside tables large enough to take bedside lamps, telephone, radio, breakfast tray, a few books... and, for the truly sybaritic, remote controls for the curtains, the angle of the bed, the television, and the lights.
If the bed occupies the middle of the room, bedside tables will be replaced by a single, long piece of furniture at the head of the bed

Use the same print for walls, curtains, and bedspread.

The shared bedroom will balance masculine and feminine elements, sober restraint with seductiveness.

A suggestion of a division between bedroom and bathroom rather than an arbitrary separation.

to accommodate all the necessary items.

— And finally an easy chair, a small table for another lamp, a bench to sit on (rather than on the bed), and a flat surface (wall-bracket or chest of drawers) onto which to empty one's pockets. When selecting these pieces, bear in mind the height of the bed. It is a disagreeable sensation to be looking up at them while lying in bed.

Ban any kind of cupboard or storage space; paradoxically, it will only get in the way. The best solution is to leave one's clothes outside the bedroom in a separate dressing room. Have nothing in the bedroom that belongs to the daytime.

The floor must be covered with a deep, soft rug or wall-to-wall carpet so that everywhere in the room you can walk barefoot.

Colour is closely linked with the occupant's personality and psychological make-up.

Blues, plums, and purples enhance a blonde complexion.

Avoid the niggardly conformism of the bedside rug.

In a warm climate, where comfort means feeling cool, you will want marble flooring, terracotta or ceramic tiles, or hand-woven cotton mats or *kilims*.

Ambience

Avoid anything aggressive, even if the decorative effect seems at first attractive. " The Crimson Bedchamber" makes an excellent title for a detective story or a film, and it is best not to rob it of its mystery!

Aim at a tranquil ambience in terms of colour, materials, and lighting.

Colour is closely linked with the occupant's personality and psychological make-up. Some people can only sleep in dark-toned surroundings; others have to have light colours.
A woman's bedroom will reflect this psychological connection between personality and colour

particularly closely. The colour of her eyes and hair, her character, activities, and emotional life will determine her environment. Goya after all used very different chromatic harmonies for the passionate Tirana and the delicate Duchess of Osuna...
Blues, plums, and purples will enhance a blonde complexion. A brunette will look her best among "furry" colours, white, and raw silk—everything that provides a contrasting, softening setting.

Dry, rough materials are out; everything should be soft, even in a man's bedroom. High-quality woolens, for example, have a velvety texture conveying a sensation of luxurious comfort to eye and touch.
Use the same print for walls, curtains, bedspreads, and chair covers. This unity will give the room balance, make it look larger than it is, and lend homogeneity to what is often a heterogeneous collection of furniture.

A more original effect can be obtained by using prints of different pattern but identical colour—like the collectors of Chinese blue wares who look for the same shade through different periods, shapes, and designs—or the other way round: the same pattern or similar patterns (stripes, for example) in different colours.

Note that today the shared bedroom is no longer predominantly feminine, as it used to be. It balances masculine and feminine elements, sober restraint with seductiveness.

A more original effect can be
obtained by using prints of different
patterns but identical colour.

XIII

For the children

In France the children's domain tends to be sacrificed to that of the grown-ups, whereas in northern Europe and in the English-speaking world the most modest house or apartment invariably includes a playroom. A child's life unfolds at a different rhythm from that of its parents', so it is important to give children a place of their own, a bedroom or playroom where they can play and express themselves without continually being told not to make too much noise and not to damage this or dirty that.

A child's world is not a childish world and you must avoid creating a design equivalent to baby talk. Children find it much more stimulating to be treated like grown-ups and to enjoy autonomy within a setting that suits them.

It is a mistake to try for the "young look" at all costs by using masses of colours and other tricks. A calm environment will foster balanced development as well as helping when it is time for homework.

Have a place where the child can draw on the wall and give his artistic impulses free rein. Children have a built-in creative urge. They should be given complete freedom in this respect.

Banish all ugliness, vulgarity, and stereotyped gadgets. Without imposing a tasteful environment (it is your taste, remember, not his), try to guide him towards what is beautiful and harmonious. But most important: let him choose for himself.

Aesthetic judgement is formed with practice, as music is best learned on a good instrument. There is nothing like an out-of-tune piano for ruining a child's ear...

The bathroom is tending to become more human. It is coming more and more to be regarded as a room to relax and enjoy oneself in.

Primarily a utility room, the bathroom is tending to become more human nowadays. It is coming more and more to be regarded as a room to relax and enjoy oneself in.

As the place where one makes one's first acquaintance with the new day, its role is also to instil a certain optimism first thing in the morning. In the evening its job is to provide the relaxation that is the essential prelude to rest.

Plan

In the average apartment the bathroom is next to the bedroom. They need not communicate directly. Access can be by a small closet that also opens onto the corridor. This kind of arrangement insulates it against circulation areas, protects it against outside noise, and heightens the feeling of privacy. As one of the "principal rooms,"

Natural lighting with, preferably, sun in the morning will put everyone in a good mood for the rest of the day.

A bathroom can be made an integral part of the bedroom.

The bathroom can
become a living
extension of the
sleeping area as such.

109

the bathroom may occasionally be even larger than the bedroom, making it a living extension of the sleeping area as such.
In the absence of a separate room, a bathroom can always be installed in an alcove or even made an integral part of the bedroom. The bedroom-bathroom gives a feeling of freedom and comfort reminiscent of the splendours of ancient Rome.

Fittings

Baths and hand-basins are often built in in such a way as to give a large flat surface on which to stand bottles, jars, and attractive toiletries. A separate shower is an added luxury. Less graceful elements—bidet and W. C.—can be concealed.

Whether standing out from the wall, set in an alcove, or even occupying the middle of the room, the bath is the star of your bathroom and offers a pretext for some surprising decorative arrangements.

Ambience

Warm materials—wood, cork, fabric, wallpaper—are no longer strangers to the bathroom. Also becoming increasingly accepted is wall-to-wall carpeting, which completely transforms the atmosphere, making the room softer and more snug. Add a fur rug for real luxury.

It is impossible to eliminate all cold materials—laminated plastic, ceramic tiles, vitrified enamel, marble, etc.—but they should be confined to areas exposed to splashing.

Powerful or dark colours are becoming to naked skin, provided you avoid reflecting certain of the more raw shades, vivid green, for example, which will take the colour out of the most golden tan.
A woman's bathroom will, like her bedroom, harmonize with her personality and with the colour of her eyes and hair—a refinement that, far from being an unattainable luxury, is the only proper setting to bring out

This kind of boudoir-bathroom can
be given a maximum of charm
without disturbing its function.

her beauty and charm. A monochrome colour scheme is preferable (monochrome having nothing to do with monotony).

Natural lighting with, preferably, sun in the morning will put everyone in a good mood for the rest of the day.
Artificial lighting must never come from the ceiling. Falling directly on the face, it will bring out the lines and tiredness in the

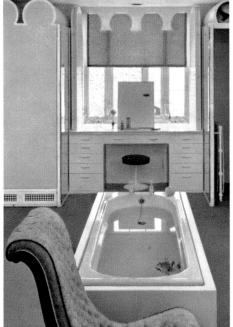

A woman's bathroom will harmonize with her personality.

features. The best solution is a mirror with a luminous frame, as used in actor's dressing rooms.

Here you can have fluorescent lighting, which comes close to natural lighting and is better for putting on make-up.

A personal note

This kind of boudoir-bathroom, a place to relax, dawdle, and day-dream in, can be given a maximum of charm without disturbing its function. One or two personal objects may suggest a particular taste or hobby:

— hang a few paintings, drawings, or serigraphs;
— exhibit some precious object that makes an unusual impression here;
— display a small collection of some kind.

The idea is not a new one: Francis I kept the finest pictures of his priceless collection in the *appartement des bains* at Fontainebleau.

Lastly, plants can transform a bathroom into a winter garden, an exotic grove in which water calls to nature... Group them by the window, or as near as possible to the source of daylight. Even more attractive is a small adjoining terrace with plants and flowers, offering a luxuriant perspective that can be reflected inside the room by means of large mirrors.

Sauna

The sauna, which is claiming more and more converts, puts the finishing touch to a well-designed sanitary complex. Easy to install, it has the additional advantage of taking up very little space.

Baths and hand-basins are often built in.

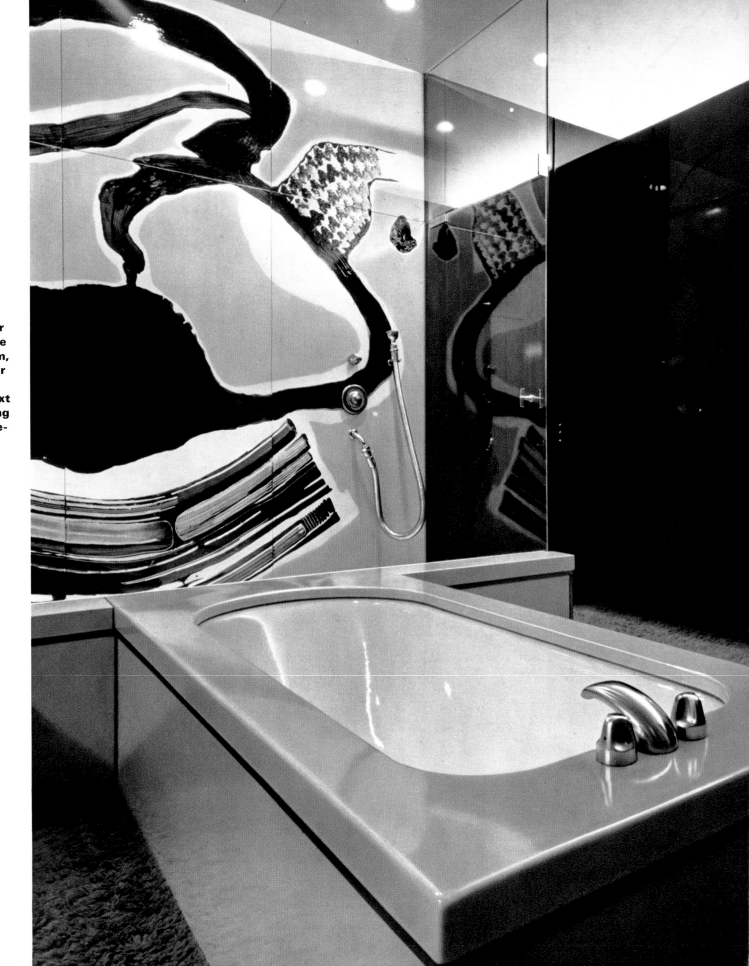

Whether standing out from the wall, set in an alcove, or even occupying the middle of the room, the bath is the star of your bathroom and offers a pretext for some surprising decorative arrangements.

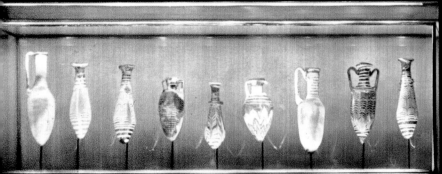

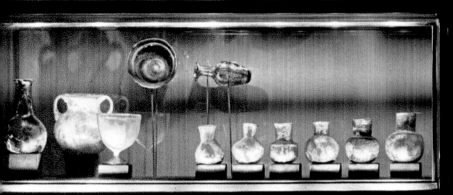

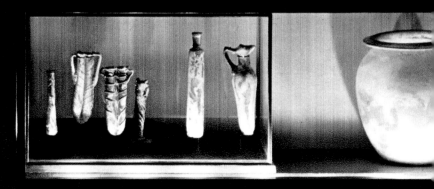

Part Three

Only buy what you like, without regard to the contingencies of fashion and speculation.

XV

Objets d'art and period furniture

Collectors

You begin by being interested, you become something of a connoisseur, and you end up a collector. Collecting has always been one of man's ways of surviving. Nowadays it is no longer a question of satisfying a passion or deepening one's knowledge of a subject by filling drawers with objects classified into sets. A new kind of collector is emerging: the cultivated modern man who likes to have around him pictures and *objets d'art* chosen with discernment, not merely in order to embellish his surroundings or for the sake of impressing other people, but because they offer him a way of expressing his personality. The collection *is* the man, sketching the secrets of his inmost being in a way that psychoanalysis can never do.

One's choice widens as one's knowledge increases. Not everyone, however, has the time or the facilities for acquiring such knowledge, in which case the best thing he can do is to have recourse to specialist, namely the antique dealer.

Antique dealers

The novice collector has an automatic distrust of antique dealers: how does he know they will not take advantage of his ignorance? This widely held assumption is overdue for revision. The antique dealer is first and foremost a connoisseur who has paid for his experience. He has taken material risks. If he makes a mistake, his investment is lost beyond recovery. The one thing he cannot allow to happen is that he should lose his reputation by exposing himself to ridicule—although ridicule is no longer as fatal as it was. The specialist who is not involved in dealing in works of art may be extremely knowledgeable, but it is all book learning. His experience is less immediate, less tactile than that of the dealer in antiques; it lacks that element of intuition, that flair, that touch that only comes from actively hunting up art treasures.

The cultivated modern man likes to have around him *objets d'art* **chosen with discernment: they offer him a way of expressing his personality.**

Quality, quite apart from the aesthetic pleasure it gives, is the safest way of evaluating a work of art.

Choosing an antique dealer

An antique dealer, like a lawyer, doctor, architect, or designer, should be chosen according to certain criteria:

— *His reputation*, which is something he either has or not...
— *His speciality*, which is his customer's guarantee of experience in the field concerned. It may be a particular period or it may be a particular article. A specialist in the eighteenth century, for example, will sell not only furniture from that period but also paintings and other objects. A specialist in ceramics, on the other hand, will cover the whole history of ceramics throughout the world; he will be able to deal in Chinese and Japanese wares as well as in Dresden, Sèvres, Chelsea, and so on.
— *His sense of taste*, which must be in harmony with that of his customer. So subtle is the relationship between them that the dealer is more than simply an adviser: he is also a friend. Like anyone who loves his job, he is delighted when someone else takes an interest in it. The businesslike approach of the collector who is interested only in making a sound investment will appeal to him less than the enthusiasm of the novice who is full of the joy of discovery and anxious to compare notes and deepen his knowledge. He will be happy to initiate anyone who knows how to listen and ask the right questions. An affinity of this kind will establish contact, facilitate communication, and lead to a more fruitful outcome.
— *Trust*, because every antique dealer is in business and consequently knows what he is about. It is childish and absurd to think that it will be an easy matter to pull a fast one on him. This kind of approach will alienate him immediately and sabotage any but the most sterile relationship of mutual deception. However paradoxical it may seem in a domain that is undoubtedly subject to the influences of fashion and speculation, the criterion of trust remains the only valid one as well as the most rewarding from every point of view.

Advice to purchasers

In both the fine and the applied arts every period, every style, and every artist enjoys a zenith. Usually it is a fairly short period—ten or fifteen years at most. Time enhances its value and works stemming from it offer the collector the surest guarantees.

Every work you buy must be an original creation, the product of an inventive mind. Avoid the copy, the pastiche, and anything that shows a lack of creative ability.

Love at first sight is something to which the most canny of collectors is not immune. Should one give in to it, with all its attendant risks and perils? Sound judgement proceeds from a cool head and a critical mind. Far from harming love, clear thinking will make sure that it lasts. So examine that coveted object coolly, calmly, and collectedly. Take it under the microscope, as it were, by placing it, as regards decoration and execution, in the context of its period. What is refinement for the seventeenth century becomes fussiness in the nineteenth because the artisan's tools as well as his whole conception and training have changed. Too much refinement diminishes. Technical prowess is no substitute for imagination.

The criteria

– *Quality*, quite apart from the aesthetic pleasure it gives, is a criterion that has stood the test of time. Together with state of preservation, it is still the safest way of evaluating a work. Quality is judged by expressiveness and by standard of execution. In furniture, for example, the eighteenth century achieved a degree of supremacy to which the mass-produced artifacts of the nineteenth century cannot aspire. Tastes change and fashion introduces new forms, but a piece that bears the maker's stamp is independent of these ephemeral contingencies. Quality never goes out of fashion.
– *Pleasantness of subject:* charm is always a good seller.

– Decorative effect: every object gains in value to the extent to which it adds to the attractiveness of your décor.

Auctions

The novice collector can learn a great deal in the auction gallery. The furniture, paintings, and *objets d'art* that come up for auction there year after year represent a cross-section of the best and worst of what is available. Experience is the best school for eye and judgement. Beware of the glamour of fashion: passing crazes lead to inflated prices. Have the courage to buy what no one is looking for yet, to rediscover what has been neglected and breathe new life into it: practise what Oscar Wilde called "creation within creation."

What to buy

Prices level off once an object or an artist has been rescued from oblivion and become known. Only exceptionally high-quality specimens will still attract big bids.

Intelligent buying means knowing the currently acceptable price for the thing you are after and being able to compare it with the price being asked. Get your information either from the expert, or from making the round of the auction galleries, or from the trade press. A selection of magazines published in different countries offers a way

Have the courage to buy what no one is looking for yet, to rediscover what has been neglected and breathe new life into it.

of arriving at an international price for certain works. This kind of investigation will reduce risks of errors of judgement and investment to a minimum.

contingencies of fashion and speculation. The greatest collectors have always been art lovers, not speculators. Time, which puts all things in their place, has sanctified their choice.

Prices

The element of financial risk, whether great or small, sharpens the collector's sense of observation. You cannot always expect to fetch a bargain, and excessive haggling is undignified. Above a certain level in the trade such practices are absurd.

Why does the more expensive piece of furniture or whatever it may be always find a buyer? Simply because knowing when to pay up is a mark of intelligence and the surest way of winning at this exciting game! Whether he will admit it or not, the most passionate collector is not blind to the investment aspect. There is nothing base about this; it is part of the game. It just must not dominate it.

To sum up, then: only buy what you like, without regard to the

The attraction a work of art lends to a décor is an added increment.

Painting and sculpture

XVI

There are various reasons for buying a painting or a piece of sculpture:

— love at first sight: you fall for the visual or intellectual pleasure it gives you, or it strikes a chord of memory or feeling;
— it possesses a decorative quality that fits well into a particular design concept;
— it completes a set or rounds off a collection;
— it strengthens your social standing by admitting you to the rank of collector and connoisseur;
— it constitutes a safe asset, offering a pretext for investment or speculation.

All these reasons are in fact valid, never mind what the aesthetes say... Indeed, it is

As far as interior design is concerned, a piece of sculpture constitutes a mass that breaks up the monotony of line and surface. It catches the light, suggesting a dynamic presence.

perfectly acceptable nowadays to associate material profit with works of the mind. Quite honestly, art for art's sake has never, as far as collectors are concerned, been anything but hypocrisy. Speculation is a driving force; the effects of snobbery can be constructive. Although in principle repugnant, this kind of mundane, financial stimulus creates interest and attracts money in the direction of art. The market, organized along rational lines, expands to include new classes of collector, and, in truth, the operation turns out to everyone's advantage. There is nothing cynical about this point of view because nobody speculates at random and without knowing exactly what he is doing. Ignorance and lack of taste lead inevitably to ruin. We are astonished and indignant when a Renoir or a Cézanne fetches some fantastic price. Yet what the price of a work of art reflects above all is a passion. And after all the work does represent the nth part of its creator's genius.

As Renoir said, "It is the collectors who make painting." Art flourishes best in powerful and prosperous nations that have reached a high degree of civilization. The ideal conditions for artistic production are a climate of luxury and a solid social order.

Investing in works of art

Firstly, an "eye" is just as important here as a "nose" and a generally receptive nature. Then you must learn—and learn by all the means at one's disposal today. You must travel; you must visit museums, galleries, and exhibitions. You must follow the specialist sales in London, Paris, New York, and elsewhere. And lastly there are books and magazines to fill out this information. This kind of global awareness of the art scene requires a certain amount of effort. The collector who claims only to like and consequently only to know anything about ancient or modern art, the Quattrocento or Cubism, is

simply lazy. He lacks the courage to go in deep enough to pick up the thread linking the most diverse creations down the centuries. The taste for intellectual speculation is more important than the taste for financial speculation. Both, however, are part of the game. For a game is what it is.

The trail-blazers of the history of art are the innovators. Long before the ordinary run of people they spot the changes taking place within society and trace fresh paths. Like all creative artists they have their zenith: a Kandinsky abstract, for example, is more valuable than his earlier Fauvist works; a work from Picabia's Dada period is a hundred times more important than his Impressionist paintings. Why? Because Abstraction and Dada constitute vital stages in the evolution of painting. Visual enjoyment is not the only criterion in art: the intellectual pleasure experienced at one remove is possibly even more important. One must see with

one's mind rather than with one's eyes alone, because behind every creation, whatever it may be, there is a man seeking to solve an enigma and share a certain sensation with his fellow-men, whether concrete (through relief, for example, by giving the surface of the canvas a third dimension) or abstract (by eliciting the same impressions as he has felt himself).

Science, technology, and psychoanalysis have thrown the best-established traditions into disarray. Artists help us to see and become aware of our changing environment. They do so by means of the continuously new techniques at their disposal. Sometimes the intention, the spontaneity of the artist's gesture count for more than the work itself.

Galleries and public auctions

The dealer's gallery serves as intermediary between artist and collector. Every artist has his dealer, and every dealer has his collectors. This triangular relationship is based on more than a mere commercial transaction.

It implies a substratum in which knowledge, love of painting, and psychology play an important role. When he buys a painting, the dealer generally knows to whom he is going to sell it. But he buys it first and foremost because he likes it. His conviction then lends weight to his financial argument. He also knows how to take risks, how to keep an artist's price bracket up if necessary or create a price bracket if none exists. His job is to get his "colts" accepted. Dealers have enabled artists of genius to emerge from obscurity.

A cluster of small sculptures can be extremely effective.

Above a certain level of quality an auction is an event on the international market. The prices paid determine future price levels. Economically they constitute a valuable index.

A particularly spectacular auction will establish a picture as a kind of listed investment. From being a work of art it becomes a Stock Exchange quotation. Frequenting auction houses is the best way of getting to know the price levels and practices of a complex market. There is only one danger—that of being tempted in the heat of the moment to bid beyond your means. It is wise to set yourself a ceiling in advance and afterwards concentrate on keeping your head and your judgement.

The place of sculpture in everyday life

Having formed an integral part of all decoration in centuries gone by and having subsequently been reduced to a minor role, sculpture is today beginning to reach a new public. Both the researches of contemporary artists and the discovery of

To live with a piece of sculpture you must find the link that ties it in with the familiar décor while at the same time enhancing its particular aura.

hitherto unknown civilizations have awakened the interest of collectors.

As far as interior design is concerned, a piece of sculpture constitutes a mass that breaks up the monotony of line and surface. It catches the light, suggesting a dynamic presence. Integrating it in its surroundings, however, raises a whole series of problems. Being a solid, it has a rhythm of its own, which must on no account clash with that of its environment.

It is not, however, necessary to create a whole room to serve as a framework for a single work of art, or to turn your apartment into a museum. To live with a piece of sculpture you must find the link that ties it in with the familiar décor while at the same time enhancing its particular aura. One of César's compressed car bodies, for example, will project dynamism into a period setting. It is a problem not of style but of structural affinity. Small pieces of sculpture from various periods and in various styles can be grouped together—

on a table, on a dresser, in a showcase, or on a bookshelf. They will set one another off either by affinity or by contrast. A cluster of small sculptures can be extremely effective.

A large piece of modern sculpture, on the other hand, simply must be exhibited in a rigorous setting against a uniform background and with plenty of space around it. A piece of sculpture standing by itself asserts its presence more successfully. Remember: the context can modify one's perception of a work of art. An eighteenth-century sculpture, for example, with its delicate curves, will take on a different meaning in a period setting than in a modern décor. On no account, however, must the setting be allowed to overrule the work.

Lighting plays a vital part here. Daylight is best, provided there is enough of it: revolving round the work, it will enhance different aspects of it with the passing

hours. If there is insufficient day-light, your artificial lighting must comply with the following principles:

— Avoid any overly harsh direct lighting: it will flatten the relief and depersonalize the work.

— Accentuate particular aspects with judiciously placed spots, but be careful not to dramatize the work to the point of altering its true meaning.

— Sculptures that were designed to be seen from below (bas-reliefs, temple statues, etc.) should also be illuminated from below.

— Remember that a sculpture in the round must be lit from every angle.

The pedestal is really a job for an expert. Certain works, however, fit better into the décor when placed directly on the floor or on a piece of furniture without any other form of support.

XVII Design

Design is a word that has become cheapened with overuse. Nowadays it is applied to everything—from the best to the worst—that aspires to modernity. It has become confused with fashion, whereas it is in fact its opposite. Design is a method by which the creator of a piece of furniture or whatever it may be is able to conceive and create it in the light not only of a particular aesthetic concept and a particular function, but also of such extremely precise factors as:

— the mechanical properties of his materials;
— modern manufacturing techniques;
— human morphology and psychology;
— economic imperatives (prices, markets, etc.).

The designer works in collaboration with the engineer, the architect, and the technician. Starting from rational data, he arrives at a coherent product that is suitably adapted to its function, to the requirements of comfort, and to the forms of everyday life. He leaves nothing out of account, neither sculptural properties nor that exclusive, living note that reveals the designer's personality.
These self-evident principles of design are not always properly understood. For example:

— Young designers have no hesitation in saying of a piece of furniture they have designed that it can be executed equally well in wood, metal, or plastic. This is nonsense. Every material has a life of its own, as César has demonstrated with his famous polystyrene castings.
— Similarly all revamping of traditional pieces of furniture in so-called modern materials—steel chests of drawers, chrome four-posters, etc.—should be banned.

Design is not a modern innovation; it arose out of the great artistic upheaval of the beginning of the century, an upheaval that affected a wide variety of disciplines from architecture and

Starting from rational data, the designer arrives at a coherent product that is suitably adapted to its function, to the requirements of comfort, and to the forms of everyday life.

137

the plastic arts to furniture, choreography, typography, and advertising. The avant-garde architects, painters, sculptors, writers, poets, and musicians of the period gave the new trends a revolutionary impetus that overthrew all the ancient canons. The most revolutionary aspect of all was the acceptance of the industrial era and of the necessity for using machines to mass-produce new artifacts different from but no less beautiful than the old craft products. Their aim was to develop a progressively leaner style, to get rid of everything that was not functionally necessary, to break with a primarily decorative aesthetic tradition. These preoccupations ought still to govern the appreciation and choice of contemporary furniture and *objets d'art*. The aesthetics of furniture are becoming more and more bound up with industrial aesthetics generally. Aeroplanes, cars, trains, ships, industrial and agricultural machinery, domestic, scientific, and cultural equipment, road signs, etc., are all, like furniture and architecture, subject to the imperatives of design. The job of artists and technicians is to put a human face on our everyday surroundings. To use the fashionable expression, they are concerned with our *environment*. Like all major problems, this positive conditioning of man by his environment is above all a question of love. Without love it will achieve nothing but the most brutally coercive of prisons.

The interior designer leaves nothing
out of account, neither sculptural
properties nor that exclusive, living
note that reveals his personality.

XVIII

Primitive arts

The criteria of quality applicable to manufactured objects or antique furniture cannot be applied to works that stem from so-called "primitive" civilizations—works of African or Oceanian art, for example, or even of pre-Columbian art. In fact, there is nothing either childish or rudimentary about primitive art. Its sculpture, pottery, and artifacts express a conception of the world that, while differing from our own, is no less rigorous. "The fetishes of Oceania and Guinea are the Christs of a different form and faith," said Apollinaire. Their style asserts itself in rhythms and volumes so foreign to the canons of our classical art as to be at first disconcerting. Their aim is not to represent—as Greek and Christian iconography sought to do—but to embody a particular significance. The African sculptor neither describes nor imitates: he refashions external reality in order to give it greater expressive force. His is an art of the intellect—the opposite of instinctive creation.

Specimens of "Negro" art were brought back from Africa by returning colonials. They were taken up by Picasso, Braque, Modigliani, and other artists and became incorporated in the art of the West. Yet it was never a question of simply copying or plagiarizing. The encounter occurred just in time to spark off fresh departures. Picasso's *Les Demoiselles d'Avignon*, Duchamp-Villon's *Horse*, and Modigliani's portraits reveal an enthusiastic search for new possibilities of expression rather than any negative return to the past. Via Cubism, Surrealism, and Abstraction, that encounter lies at the origin of the fascinating adventure of modern art. In fact, it is exactly as if the great currents of art were subject, beyond time and space, to certain universal archetypes inherent in man's make-up. The true creators all follow identical paths. The collector who buys a Warega mask or a Baoulé fetish "because it makes him think of Picasso, or Giacometti" is referring it to his own culture; at the same time,

"Primitive" sculpture, pottery, and artifacts express a conception of the world that, while differing from our own, is no less rigorous.

The African sculptor neither describes nor imitates. He refashions external reality in order to give it greater expressive force.

however, he is testifying to the universality of art. Such cross-references can be found in all the great collections.

The market

Artists were the pioneers, as they always have been. They created the fashion for primitive art, which in turn created a market.

Nevertheless the reservations of the public at large were not removed until 1959 when a primitive statue, sold by auction, fetched the same kind of price as works of classical art. This extraordinary increase in value is of course confined to pieces of exceptional quality. The very much more numerous works of middling quality remain fairly stable and may even be difficult to sell.

Aesthetic quality, then, determines up to 95% of the value of a piece of African or Oceanian sculpture. Collectors attach greater importance to the work itself than to its place of origin, wherever that may be.

The criteria of appreciation

There are good and bad sculptors in Africa and Oceania, as there are in Europe. Nor are they all necessarily anonymous. If the social structures of the day do not always make it possible to identify names, they cannot prevent the connoisseur from recognizing a particular hand, and sometimes—very occasionally—an expert is able to trace a connection.

Date is not an essential criterion. The most important works, however, definitely stem from the period between 150 and 300 years ago. Works dating from after the penetration of European influence lack the expressive force of their earlier counterparts. Under pressure of a blind if not destructive Christianity, their sacred character disappeared. They became stereotyped, losing their incantatory aura and with it all claim to our attention.

The often artificial patina (based on palm oil) on primitive works makes little difference to an appreciation of their quality.

In small, hand-worked objects, wonderfully impregnated, the material is in fact enhanced. In other cases it is the patina of time, the scaly tarnish forming a rough surface that may be much sought after.

The important things are:

— the arrangement of architectural rhythms and masses;
— lines that are alive and expressive, yet always controlled. Even a static work must never be stiffly rigid;
— the way the wood is worked, i.e., the sculptor's skill in turning knots and the direction and density of the grain to advantage.

But the best way to set about building up a collection is to rely on the expert. His job, we repeat, is not merely to sell but also to offer guidance. His experience—often gained in the field or, as in this case, the jungle with all its risks and perils—is the best guarantee. It will save the collector from the errors of an uncertain judgement.

What counts is lines that are alive and expressive, yet always controlled. Even a static work must never be stiffly rigid.

Ambience has to do with an intimate feeling of well-being, a deep, organic harmony between man and his environment.

Part Four

XIX

Choosing an ambience

It is important not to confuse *ambience* with *décor*, as is too commonly done. Whatever is attractive, external, or artificial comes under the heading of décor. Ambience, on the other hand, has to do with a feeling of well-being, a deep, organic harmony between man and his environment. Every ambience suggests a life-style; it "psychoanalyses" its occupant's personality. Sometimes, too, the premises will impose directives, commanding respect or drawing attention to certain peculiarities. The interior designer's job is to strike a balance between these internal and external motivations in order to create a setting that is both psychically and physically good to live in.

The classical ambience

Every classical ambience has reference to the past, either in a spirit of reconstruction or in a spirit of adaptation:

— *Reconstruction* is admissible only within an adequate frame-

The problem here is one not of recreating a period setting but of transforming it without impairing its essential flavour.

147

work, i.e., in period dwellings whose interior design is the key to the whole arrangement. In such cases—and they are pretty rare—one has to draw on contemporary documents to find out how things were originally. The requirements of comfort—heating, sanitation—must involve no visible sacrifices. The personality of the occupant will find expression in the choice and quality of the elements—furniture, pictures, *objets d'art*—rather than in their arrangement, this being subject to precise conventions.

— *Adaptation* of a particular style allows greater freedom. The problem here is one not of recreating a period setting but of transforming it without impairing its essential flavour. On the basis of knowledge of authentic elements, look for equivalents—materials, colours, objects—in a more modern, more diversified vein.

It is also perfectly admissible to introduce modern elements into a period context. Such a mar-riage of ancient and modern must be entered into without prejudice, the sole common criterion being quality. The joiners and cabinet-makers of the seventeenth and eighteenth centuries had the same concern for form and the same feeling for proportion as designers today. There is nothing improper about placing their creations side by side. The major innovation as far as seating is concerned is a new sense of comfort. We like to sit lower down nowadays, to sprawl... The antique armchair implies a more dignified posture. Still, if well conceived and designed, it is no less comfortable.

The contemporary ambience

This taste for comfort, which often determines the choice of a contemporary ambience, does not rule out the possibility of aesthetic pleasure.
Simplify the structure of the room as much as you can. Get rid of everything that spoils the lines of the architecture—mould-

Simplify the structure of the room as much as you can. Get rid of everything that spoils the lines of the architecture.

ings, cornices, fake panelling, dummy windows, etc.—in short, of every element of artifice. This severity, indispensable to begin with, will subsequently be tempered by the play of contrasting materials with their suggestion of life and dynamism. The contrast will only work, however, with a limited number of materials.

Avoid:

— everything that is not necessary to the life of the occupants;
— objects divested of their proper functions: the place for folklore is in the museum;
— any kind of pastiche of materials or authentic elements: polystyrene beams, electric log-fires, etc.;
— everything small, mean, impractical, and uncomfortable. Padding is the antithesis of comfort.

As Proust said, "The foundation-stone of a good drawing room is sacrifice."

Decorative elements

A collection may be the key to an ambience: old masters or modern paintings, drawings, pieces of sculpture, primitive art objects, weapons, trophies, etc. The theme will vary with the personality of the occupant, revealing his deepest predilections. To love things is to want to bring them to life. Avoid a systematic, over-finicky arrangement. Successful presentation will give an impression of freedom and simplicity. The casual touch gives greater charm than originality at any price. A few guide lines will suffice to put order into this apparent disorder:

Objets d'art:

Find out by experiment the kind of associations that heighten the beauty of a particular form or material. Tucked away in a glass cabinet, your Renaissance bronze is just a sad little knick-knack. Placed near a modern painting, it will recover its identity.
Rather than spreading out pieces that individually offer no special attraction, it is better to group them together. Accumulation has a striking effect, as a number of contemporary artists have shown—Arman, in particular, or think of Andy Warhol with his Coca-Cola bottles.

Objects of the most diverse origins, techniques, and inspirations can be placed together. The thing is to find the common denominator—quality, period, material, certain criteria that coincide exactly in what appear to be very different civilizations.

Paintings:

The right height to hang a painting is at eye-level, or even a little below, since a slightly lowered horizon creates a more intimate atmosphere.
When arranged horizontally in one or more rows, paintings of different sizes should be aligned by their upper or lower edges. Arranged vertically on a narrow strip of wall or a pillar, they can be aligned by one side.
When hanging pictures above a piece of furniture, take into account the volume of the latter so that the whole shall be harmoniously proportioned.
Depending on the particular case, the pictures can be hung in a discreet geometrical arrangement —circle, oval, square, or rectangle—which should rarely be allowed to extend beyond the limits of the piece of furniture

To love things is to want to bring them to life. Find out by experiment the kind of associations that heighten the beauty of a particular form or material.

151

concerned. Large- and small-format pictures go perfectly well together, with the alignments occasionally intersecting. We repeat: avoid any kind of systematic or conventional bias, the important thing being to satisfy eye and mind...

The frame can modify the attractiveness of a work either for better or for worse. An original, unashamedly Baroque frame and a mediocre painting may make a charming combination.
Modern paintings look best in plain, narrow frames. A good drawing, engraving, or lithograph generally needs no more than a piece of glass with a mount in a colour that harmonizes. In some cases a worn antique moulding will heighten by contrast the aura of a modern work, lending it a special charm.

The isolated decorative element:

A large-scale work such as a statue is a mass standing in space. It must be placed with due regard to the masses of the pieces of furniture standing around it in order to avoid "crushing" it. Remember that lighting, whether natural or artificial, is of the greatest importance in setting off a large piece of sculpture.

Add the kind of natural element so essential to a sane environment by creating a little indoor garden in a tub or a series of pots or troughs.

XX Plants and winter gardens

A "nature corner" is fast becoming a necessity in an increasingly artificial existence. A mass of flowers or greenery filling a corner of the living room lends a note of reverie, offering escape into another, more exotic, world... This indoor garden can be arranged in a variety of ways:

— on the ground floor it can form part of the floor itself, when this is provided for architecturally;
— alternatively it can be accommodated in a large tub or in a group of smaller tubs or troughs.

Above all avoid the kind of stiff arrangement that gives flowers that sad, Sunday look... Aim instead at something like a natural rockgarden with its grasses and ferns and little clumps of flowers, or a jungle of giant foliage and tangled creepers.
Provide a single light source—a spot on the floor, for example—for the evening, to pick out the structure of your plants and throw exciting shadows.

A winter garden is a more complex affair needing a terrace or a fairly large balcony. If the plan of the premises makes it impossible to build a proper loggia, it is important at least to keep the wind off by means of glass or plexiglass walls up to the height of a man. Your plants will then have the advantages of sun and fresh air without the disadvantages of chilly drafts.
The nurseryman or landscape gardener must think like an architect in balancing mass and colour, light and shadow...
But he must also be a poet if his winter garden—however tiny—is miraculously to take on the dimensions of a dream. Here too mirrors have a part to play.
A fountain, a small pond, or even a swimming pool will add that naturalistic element so essential to every dream. Choose plain, matching garden furniture —of white-painted wood or metal, cane, Manilla, or bamboo —and one colour only for your awning, sun mats, and seat cushions in order to avoid any hint of garishness.

A mass of flowers or greenery filling a corner of the living room lends a note of reverie, offering escape into another, more exotic world.

A winter garden needs a terrace or fairly large balcony.

Choose plain, matching garden furniture.

One colour only for the seat cushions in order to avoid garishness.

A "nature corner"
is fast becoming
a necessity in an
increasingly artificial
existence.

The nurseryman or
landscape gardener
must think like an
architect in balancing
mass and colour,
light and shadow.

A fountain, a small pond, or even a swimming pool will add that naturalistic element so essential to every dream.

A winter garden must also be the work of a poet if the space it occupies—however tiny—is miraculously to take on the dimensions of dream.

Acknowledgments and list of interior decorators

The photos are numbered from left to right and from top to bottom

Page	Photographer	Interior decorator	Page	Photographer	Interior decorator
2, 3	Reinhart Wolf	Peter Preller	33	Marc Lavriller	Carla Venosta
6, 7	Marc Lavriller	Alain Demachy	34	Marc Lavriller	F. Catroux
11	Carla de Benedetti	Claudio Dini	35	Marc Lavriller	Gae Aulenti
13 (1)	Marianne Haas	Alain Demachy	36 (1)	Pierre Berdoy	David Hicks
13 (2)	Marc Lavriller	Jacques Grange	36 (2)	Trintignan	M. de Potestad
13 (3)	Marianne Haas	Alain Demachy	37	Marc Lavriller	C. de Sevigny
15	Marianne Haas	Michel Boyer	39 (1)	Marianne Haas	Alain Demachy
17 (1)	Carla de Benedetti	Claudio Dini	39 (2)	Marc Lavriller	Alain Demachy
17 (2)	Marc Lavriller		40 (1)	Marc Lavriller	Peter Halden
17 (3)	Marc Lavriller	Albrizzi	40 (2)	Marianne Haas	Michel Boyer
19 (1)	Marianne Haas	Alain Demachy	40 (3)	Marc Lavriller	F. Catroux
19 (2)	Marianne Haas	Alain Demachy	40 (4)	Marianne Haas	Alain Demachy
20 (1)	Marianne Haas	Jacques Grange	41	Marianne Haas	Alain Demachy
20 (2)	Trintignan	C. de Sevigny	43 (1)	Marianne Haas	Alain Demachy
21	Marianne Haas	Alain Demachy	43 (2)	Marianne Haas	Michel Boyer
22 (1)	Marc Lavriller	Carla Venosta	44	Marc Lavriller	
22 (2)	Marc Lavriller	Gae Aulenti	45 (1)	Marianne Haas	Alain Demachy
23	Carla de Benedetti		45 (2)	Pierre Berdoy	David Hicks
25 (1)	Marc Lavriller	Badenberg	46 (1)	Marianne Haas	Jacques Grange
25 (2)	Marc Lavriller	Badenberg	46 (2)	Marianne Haas	Alain Demachy
25 (3)	Marianne Haas	Jacques Grange	46 (3)	Peter Bermbach	René Gruau
26 (1)	Trintignan	M. de Potestad	46 (4)	Marianne Haas	A. Demachy, A. Julia
26 (2)	Marc Lavriller	C. de Sevigny	47 (1)	Marianne Haas	Alain Demachy
27 (1)	Marianne Haas	Michel Boyer	47 (2)	Marianne Haas	Alain Demachy
27 (2)	Carla de Benedetti		48 (1)	Marianne Haas	Jacques Grange
29	Carla de Benedetti		48 (2)	Pierre Berdoy	C. de Sevigny
31	Carla de Benedetti		48 (3)	Marc Lavriller	David Hicks
32	Carla de Benedetti		49 (1)	Marianne Haas	Alain Demachy

Page	Photographer	Interior decorator
49 (2)	Marianne Haas	Alain Demachy
49 (3)	Marianne Haas	Alain Demachy
51	Carla de Benedetti	Bicocchi, Monsani
52	Marianne Haas	
53 (1)	Marianne Haas	M. de Potestad
53 (2)	Marianne Haas	Jacques Grange
53 (3)	J. Dussart	Alain Demachy
54 (1)	Marc Lavriller	Howard Symmons
54 (2)	Marianne Haas	Alain Demachy
55	Marc Lavriller	Albrizzi
57	Carla de Benedetti	Gae Aulenti
58 (1)	Marc Lavriller	David Hicks
58 (2)	Marianne Haas	Alain Demachy
59 (2)	Carla de Benedetti	Carla Venosta
61	Marianne Haas	Alain Demachy
63 (1)	Marianne Haas	Alain Demachy
63 (2)	Marc Lavriller	C. de Sevigny
63 (3)	Marianne Haas	Alain Demachy
64 (1)	Marianne Haas	Alain Demachy
64 (2)	Marianne Haas	Alain Demachy
64 (3)	Marianne Haas	Alain Demachy
66 (1)	Carla de Benedetti	Piero Catellini
66 (2)	Pierre Berdoy	David Hicks
66 (3)	Pierre Berdoy	Badenberg
67 (1)	Marc Lavriller	
67 (2)	Marianne Haas	Alain Demachy
69 (1)	Marianne Haas	Alain Demachy
69 (2)	Marianne Haas	Alain Demachy
71 (1)	Marc Lavriller	C. de Sevigny
71 (2)	Marianne Haas	Alain Demachy
71 (3)	Marianne Haas	Alain Demachy
72, 73	Marianne Haas	Alain Demachy
75	Marianne Haas	Alain Demachy
77	Marianne Haas	Alain Demachy
78 (1)	Marianne Haas	Alain Demachy
78 (2)	Marianne Haas	Alain Demachy
79	Marianne Haas	Alain Demachy
80	Reinhart Wolf	Peter Preller
82	Marianne Haas	Alain Demachy
83	Marianne Haas	Alain Demachy
85	Marianne Haas	Alain Demachy
86 (1)	Marc Lavriller	Gae Aulenti
86 (2)	E. Woodman	Barry Broadbert
87 (1)	Marianne Haas	Jacques Grange
87 (2)	Marianne Haas	Roselyne Franck
89 (1)	Marc Lavriller	F. Catroux
89 (2)	Marianne Haas	Alain Demachy
90 (1)	Marianne Haas	Alain Demachy
90 (2)	Marc Lavriller	C. de Sevigny
91	Marianne Haas	Alain Demachy
93 (1)	Marianne Haas	Alain Demachy
93 (2)	Marianne Haas	Alain Demachy
93 (3)	Marianne Haas	Alain Demachy
94 (1)	Carla de Benedetti	Claudio Dini
94 (2)	Marianne Haas	Alain Demachy
95 (1)	Frank Beyda	Fourcade
95 (2)	Marianne Haas	Roselyne Franck
97 (1)	Marianne Haas	Jacques Grange
97 (2)	Carla de Benedetti	Carla Venosta
99	Marc Lavriller	David Hicks
100 (1)	Pierre Berdoy	C. de Sevigny
100 (2)	Marc Lavriller	C. de Sevigny
101 (1)	Pierre Berdoy	C. de Sevigny
101 (2)	Pierre Berdoy	David Hicks
101 (3)	J. Dussart	Alain Demachy
102	Marianne Haas	Michel Boyer
103 (1)	Carla de Benedetti	
103 (2)	Marianne Haas	Alain Demachy
105 (1)	Marc Lavriller	C. de Sevigny
105 (2)	Michael Boys	David Hicks
107	Michael Boys	Douglas Norwood
108 (1)	Marc Lavriller	Jacques Grange
108 (2)	Marianne Haas	P. Barbe
109	Marc Lavriller	M. de Potestad
111	Marc Lavriller	David Hicks
112 (1)	J. Dussart	Alain Demachy
112 (2)	Pierre Berdoy	David Hicks
113 (1)	Marianne Haas	Alain Demachy
113 (2)	Frank Beyda	
115 (1)	Marianne Haas	M. de Potestad
115 (2)	Marc Lavriller	C. de Sevigny
115 (3)	Marc Lavriller	Gae Aulenti

Page	Photographer	Interior decorator
115 (4)	Marianne Haas	A. Champalle
115 (5)	Carla de Benedetti	Claudio Dini
115 (6)	Marianne Haas	Alain Demachy
115 (7)	Carla de Benedetti	Claudio Dini
116	Marc Lavriller	H. Samuel
117	Carla de Benedetti	Nandavigo
118, 119	Marianne Haas	Alain Demachy
121	Marianne Haas	Alain Demachy
122	Marianne Haas	Alain Demachy
123	Marianne Haas	Alain Demachy
125 (1)	Marc Lavriller	Alain Demachy
125 (2)	Pierre Berdoy	David Hicks
127	Marianne Haas	Alain Demachy
128	Marianne Haas	Alain Demachy
131 (1)	Marianne Haas	Alain Demachy
131 (2)	Marianne Haas	Alain Demachy
132	Marianne Haas	Alain Demachy
133	Marianne Haas	
135	Marianne Haas	Alain Demachy
137	Carla de Benedetti	Gae Aulenti
139	Carla de Benedetti	Pes & Federici
141	Marianne Haas	Alain Demachy
142	Marianne Haas	Alain Demachy
143	Marianne Haas	A. Demachy, A. Julia
144, 145	Marianne Haas	Alain Demachy
147	Marianne Haas	D. Aaron, A. Demachy
149	Carla de Benedetti	Carla Venosta
151	Marianne Haas	Alain Demachy
153	Marianne Haas	Alain Demachy
155	Marianne Haas	Jacques Grange
156 (1)	Marc Lavriller	Alain Demachy
156 (2)	Marc Lavriller	C. de Sevigny
156 (3)	Pierre Berdoy	C. de Sevigny
157	Marianne Haas	Alain Demachy
158 (2)	Marc Lavriller	C. de Sevigny
159 (1)	Marianne Haas	Alain Demachy
159 (2)	Marianne Haas	A. Demachy, A. Julia

The text of this book, the four-colour offset illustrations and jacket, and the heliogravure reproductions were printed in June 1974 by Roto-Sadag S.A., Geneva. – Photolithos by Atesa Argraf S.A., Chêne-Bourg/Geneva. – The binding is by Schumacher S.A., Schmitten. – Editorial: Dominique Guisan. – Production: Suzanne Meister.

Printed in Switzerland